* * *

RESCUING
VANISHING
MANHOOD

Hope for Healing Unfathered Men

Joseph Oblinger

* * *

LIFEVEST PUBLISHING, INC.
Centennial, CO

to

Tom, Mark, Dan, & John

◇◇

Published and printed by:
LifeVest Publishing
4901 E. Dry Creek Rd., #170
Centennial, CO 80122
www.lifevestpublishing.com

Printed in the United States of America

ISBN 1-59879-561-9

TABLE OF REFLECTIONS

FOREWARD

Over the course of the years of my ministry, whether as a priest, as a counselor, or as a spiritual director, I became more and more aware of the issues raised in this book. They have been deep concerns for me, and I kept asking myself, "why doesn't somebody do something about this?" On the edges of my consciousness I kept hearing "why don't you write a book?" - a frequent injunction that came from men at our workshops and retreats. Writing a book, at that time, appeared to be such a monumental undertaking, for which I did not seem to have the talent, nor the time. Now that I have had the experience of producing a credible manuscript, namely "Fisher of Men," my autobiography, this new effort hasn't seemed such a daunting task.

This is not a scientific study based on anecdotal evidence or case studies of persons over the years, or basic principles of sociology or psychology. This is a series of reflections, personal reactions to the events that have occurred around me, or as I have witnessed them through the variety of our modern communication technologies.

During the early 1980's, sparked by Robert Bly's book, "Iron John," a wealth of published material about masculine issues began to appear. Whether this was the result of the women's movement that emerged in the previous decade remains a possibility.

Inspired by the work of Henri J. M. Nouwen, I began to gather materials and develop approaches to the identification and healing of my sick brothers that live on the planet. The issues are not parochial or regional, but universal across the planet. In spite of the noble efforts of a number of authors twenty years ago, little seems to have emerged on the scene to address this issue in a practical way. There were numerous "should do steps" suggested along the way, but little in the way of practical, hands on, well integrated programs. It would seem that our current culture is in a state of denial.

Many years ago, I was introduced to the manhood issues in a priests' retreat directed by Father Richard Rohr, a Franciscan who currently directs a program in Albuquerque, called "Action and Contemplation."

In the onset of the new century, John Eldridge emerged with his book, "Wild at Heart," which became immediately popular among Evangelical Christians. It touched the deepest longings and anxieties of the man in our culture today. John did not just write about the issue, but he instituted a program to bring awareness and healing to the broken spirits of many men. These sessions became very popular and have ministered to thousands, demonstrating the need for such programs.

I do not claim to be an expert, but an observer sensitive to the pain and frustration of so many men in our culture today. Through my study and my ministry to men, I may now have acquired some credentials in social psychology as I try to identify the roots of this sickness, which perhaps only the AIDS/HIV pandemic surpasses in its universality. It ranks up there with the problem of global warming. Even these issues may be tied to the subject matter of this reflection.

My intention in pursuing this issue is simply to raise the question once again, to encourage reflection and dialog among the various disciplines dealing with both individual and social behavior. By pursuing this, we may come up with some methodologies and therapies, similar to Eldridge's, to stem the tide of all the destructive consequences of fatherlessness.

When I began this undertaking, my intent was to be as objective as possible. I quickly became aware that

I could not ignore my own history and the parameters within which I must work, particularly that of my Christian faith. Consequently, I present this project flavored with views and aspects of my faith, lived out within the Roman Catholic community.

I am well aware of the fact that some folks will disagree with some of my reflections. I may not always be "politically correct." But I don't think politics should have anything to do with these very serious social and moral problems. My wish is that folks will begin to think about these ideas, enter into discussions about them thereby bringing them out into the open where they can be dealt with in rational and positive ways.

In concluding their book, "Warrior, King, Magician, Lover," Moore and Gillette comment *". . . at this time it is clear that the world is overpopulated with not only immature men, but also tyrannical and abusive little girls pretending to be women. It is time for men, particularly men of Western civilization, to stop accepting the blame for everything that is wrong in the world . . . the enemy for both genders is not the other one but infantile grandiosity and the splitting of the self that results from it. "*[1]

On occasions when I have shared the subject matter of this work with others, I have noted the nods of approval, especially from the ladies in the audience. I know that this is a concern for a lot of people in the world and that gave me the courage to proceed.

---

1   Robert Moore & Douglas Gillette, "Warrior, King, Magician, Lover" pp.155-6

OPENING REFLECTION

Entering into this search for the causes and reasons for what we perceive as a vanishing manhood, we need to establish some environmental aspects of today's world that will govern our search. Certain sociological and theological givens will offer the parameters within which I will have to carry on this investigation.

THE CALL TO HOLINESS

We live in an increasingly complicated world. Two hundred years ago Thomas Jefferson was president of the United States and rode around on horseback or in a carriage of some kind. Horsepower was the means of transportation. The Corps of Discovery was launched with little crafts powered by wind and human back power. Mail took days to get from sender to addressee.

One hundred years later Theodore Roosevelt was president – the youngest ever. John F. Kennedy missed the record by one year. The San Francisco quake and fire occurred one hundred years ago. At the end of the nineteenth century America was launched into the techno-age by the inventions of Thomas A. Edison. Since then, think of all of the scientific explorations and discoveries of the last 100 years that have catapulted us into the "technological age" of television, computers, cell-phones, i-pods, and i-phones. This is a phenomenon that is both awe inspiring and frightening. Yes, think of all the gadgets and appliances you take for granted that did not exist when you came into this world. As civilization moved forward, life and living became more complex.

It is in the midst of such a complex world that religious folks are called to believe and to live. That, of course, has always been the case. In Jefferson's milieu, for example, everyone was a Christian and generally held to Christian values, although terribly divided. By the time Teddy Roosevelt assumed the presidency, the great migrations from Europe were beginning and adding to the ethnic and religious diversity of the growing republic. Already in the Second Vatican Council, the fathers of that historic gathering faced this new and complex world with their document "Constitution on the Church in the Modern World" (Gaudium et Spes). It was a detour from the set agenda of the organizers of the council. This was perceived to have been a profound movement of the Holy Spirit forcing the Church to see the complexity of its relationship to all that was going on in the world society at the time.

Forty years ago, this international gathering of the shepherds of the Catholic Church provided us with a vision for the Church, and for the individual Christian who would live into the twenty-first century. The overriding call was simply "be holy as your Father is holy!" (Matt. 5:48)

The most important aspect of church renewal is the conversion of the human heart, the renewal of each baptized person. The call to holiness is the most important and overriding aspect of any renewal effort.

The entire pontificate of John Paul II was clearly focused on these challenges. No one took the teachings of the council more seriously than he did. He spoke to these issues often and in great detail, especially those surrounding this "call to holiness." And what is more, he lived it out in his own personal life. For the listening and fervent Christian there is no way we could have escaped that call. Certainly there are those, all too few, who have made the effort, not only to live that vision, but to help others do likewise.

As time went on, we allowed ourselves to drift away from the articles of faith by which Christians have believed and lived for these two thousand years. More and more we seem to allow the world of the flesh to set our agenda and to inspire our behavior. What has happened is that we have become so secularized that we have forgotten we live in two worlds – the world we can see and a world we cannot see - the world of the spirit. And both are important to our well-being. More and more we find ourselves rooted in the world of the here and now, with our hearts, minds and feelings mired in the muck of a meaningless existence. We live as though there is no other world than the one we can see. The consequences of this rebellion is so evident around us today. Everywhere we look, everything we hear tends to have a negative, destructive aspect to it. Even the good things that occur are too often diluted by greed and selfishness. What the ancients of our faith were able to do, which the modern Christian has great difficulty in doing, is creating a balance between being of the world and being of the spirit. And that really is what holiness is all about. In using the word, "holiness," one may think of it only in terms of piety or devotion. We use it here, however, in the sense of human wholeness, the seeking and struggling to become a well-integrated human being.

Recall that Jesus once challenged his followers, those fishermen, "to be perfect as your heavenly Father is perfect!" (Matt. 5:48). What did he mean by that? Are we to become like God? Well, in a way, yes, but not in the way one might think. God is perfect because he fulfills the purpose of his being, his existence. We are called to fulfill the nature and purpose of our existence…to be truly human persons. To be human is to be fully what God intended you to be from the beginning, to be his image in the world, to be the reflection of his goodness to the seen world. St. Irenaeus phrased it this way: "The glory of God is man fully alive." (cf. Irenaeus...) Anything short of that, of course, is to be inhuman or anti-human. That is what sin really is: not fulfilling your destiny, not being Godly - not being HOLY. It is the holy person who is quite comfortable in both worlds - the world of the flesh and the world of the spirit. We have countless examples of this balance in the lives of the saints.

To be one in Christ is to be united in heart and mind and spirit, to be community. What was it Jesus said at his Last Supper? "Men will come to believe because of your love for one another." That is "solidarity." The whole point here is to provide a backdrop against which we can examine both the historical and spiritual dimensions of the subject of this book: fatherlessness, manhood. As we will discover, there is no solution to any of the monumental problems that face mankind today, nor even many personal problems without God and without his revelation.

It is a time to reenter the lost world of the Spirit, a time to reunite our two worlds in the balance of serenity and hope, giving solid meaning to the journey that each one is upon. Yes, this life is not an end in itself, but only a lap in the journey to our ultimate end, life with the Father for ever and ever and ever. What does that mean? We simply do not know. Recall what Paul wrote to his believers in Corinth: "...what eye has not seen, and ear has not heard, and what has not entered the human heart, what God has prepared for those who love him..." (1 Cor. 2:9)

The road to holiness is a long process. It isn't something that happens overnight or spontaneously. There will be a lot of battles to be fought along the way, many stages to go through. For the male, the very first prerequisite is to be a beloved son.

SPIRIUALITY OF SONSHIP

The journey into the deep masculine or manhood begins by being the son. We see this emphasis on sonship in the gospel stories about Jesus himself. In the beginning of his ministry he is baptized in the Jordan by John the Baptist, and during that ritual we hear the Father's voice: "This is my beloved son in whom I am well pleased." (Matt. 3:17) What is this, if not a rite of passage, as we view Jesus moving from the comfort of his home with Mary and Joseph to the ministry he has been sent to accomplish.

Two years later, we hear that same voice during the Transfiguration on Mt. Tabor, but with a little different twist: "This is my beloved Son. Listen to him!" (Matt 17:5) Here we have another passage event from his ministry of teaching and healing to that of deep loving and sacrifice.

In preparation for this important aspect of his vocation, Jesus teaches his disciples about sonship in the fifth chapter of John's Gospel. "Amen, amen, I say to you, a son cannot do anything on his own but only what he sees his father doing; for what he does his son will do also!" (John 5:19). Here Jesus, on another level, seems to be pointing to the basic spirituality of the male. Christian spirituality for the masculine is the spirituality of sonship; the spirituality of the feminine is essentially "bridal" or nupturient spirituality. In understanding this distinction we can begin to appreciate that the means of growing spiritually in the Christian life, the road to holiness, will be different for men than it will be for women.

What seems to be our purpose here is a focus on the anthropological aspects of the male, i.e., what were the primal qualities or characteristics of manhood as he came from the hand of the creator? What is it that makes a man to be truly man? A father? A leader? What is it that makes a son to be truly son?

According to the psychologist Carl Jung, there is within each human person a vast reservoir of memories secreted into the depths of our unconscious world – not just memories of events and people of our personal biography, but memories of our history as a race, the human species on this planet. Where do we access these primal memories, we might ask? Actually, through our dreams and imagination. Poetry, art, music, and story telling are fruits of the imagination. Should we not then go to this source for our insights into human nature? In our recent experience we have been introduced to the *Lord of the Rings* and to the *Chronicles of Narnia*. Both C. S. Lewis and J. R. R. Tolkien were imaginative story tellers. Both of them were able to weave, although quite subtly, into their stories, deep Christian themes.

We can also recall and examine the old myths, the fables, and the fairy tales of our earliest days of childhood. These stories in turn are repeated and dressed up in modern stories we find in novels and movies. What can they tell us that help to answer these questions?

A few years ago the work of John Eldridge was brought to my attention. John is a Christian author and counselor. From him we have learned some very insightful facts about maleness, especially in regards to the father-son relationship. His approach is rooted in what we have just been describing – the exploration of myths and stories that are deeply rooted in the psyche. In his book, "Wild at Heart," he suggests that men should recall their favorite movies or stories, which in turn will suggest the qualities and characteristics of maleness. His recent ministry for men has had phenomenal success touching the lives of thousands of men from all over the world.

He attacks head on the fatherlessness of our culture. Against the background of the Colorado wilderness, he invites men to spend several sessions exploring their own relationship with their fathers and also their relationship with their sons.

Sonship presumes a father is not simply biological but has a social and psychological role as well. The father's role in the life of his sons, and his daughters as well, is essential during the entire growing process. The older the child gets the more important the father's role becomes.

No longer can this occur automatically as it once did when we lived in an agrarian world. In a culture that has gradually eroded the values and meaning of family and loyalty, it will take a supreme amount of strength and perseverance to achieve any kind of healthy relationship between a father and his children.

CLEAN UP THE LANGUAGE

Choosing the right words to say what one really wants to say is one of the most difficult aspects of writing. One wants his or her message to be unambiguous, so that it will be clear to the average reader. In the culture we live in today, euphemisms are constantly being employed to mask the truth, or to confuse the issue.

Recently, there appeared a piece from the Associated Press in Washington D.C. entitled "Doublespeak." The article stated - "In Washington words are a moving target that conceal at least as much as they reveal." They quote a study, from the Cato Institute, that took on the rising tide of fuzzy words in our fight against terrorism, arguing that whatever the people think of what the government is doing, it would help to understand what the government really is doing.

These are some of the examples they came up with. Suicide by captives was called "a self-injurious behavior incident." Interrogations are "debriefings." How could any one possibly oppose the "Patriot Act" and still be a patriot?

One of the areas where euphemisms play an indispensable role is in the area of human sexuality. The issues here have become so complex, it is very hard sometimes to know just exactly what is being said. Take, for example, the abortion issue. No Democrat would use the word, abortion, it's too negative. The "right to choose" replaces abortion in any discussion involving liberals (now progressives). Such words are used either to disguise or obliterate the facts, or the reality. No matter what you call it, the woman who chooses "abortion" - the termination of a human life – is responsible for a homicide.

The problem with the whole "Pro Choice" mentality is in its far reaching consequences. Most of the evils surrounding marriage and family life today can be rooted in "Pro Choice." Have you not observed how many new-born babies have been dumped into garbage cans or flushed down the toilet; or how many young children have been destroyed by a mother who found them inconvenient? This theology or philosophy of convenience has infiltrated all aspects of our culture today. A marriage becomes inconvenient, so we kill it with a divorce. A fellow student becomes inconvenient, so I bring a gun to school and liberate myself from this inconvenience.

The same thing holds true at the end of life as well. Pain and suffering, or even old age itself, is mighty inconvenient. Why should anyone have to endure that? Why not euthanasia? This all has to do with control! Who or what really is in charge of life? The answer to such a question is hard to come by, unless we are aware of some very deep and fundamental changes that have taken place in our culture today. Let us briefly look at this.

Real knowledge and understanding comes to us in three different ways: through our feeling or gut; through our reason; or through our faith. Feeling speaks to our emotional response to reality; reason speaks to our intellectual comprehension of reality; and faith speaks to our spiritual knowing of reality. For a balanced approach in our connection with reality, all three should be playing their role. When we look at reality through only one of these lenses, what we get is a warped view of that reality.

Up until the thirteenth century reality was seen pretty much in faith terms, though primitive before Abraham, but after Christ it eventually blossomed into what was called, "the greatest of centuries," because Christendom reigned supreme, at least in the West. At the same time this century gave birth to the influence of reason or intelligence in the endeavor to understand reality. It was then that we began to have the struggle between faith and science – the great conflicts surrounding the understanding of the universe – Copernicus and Galileo, who were challenging the exclusive faith tradition about the world in which we live. This struggle between faith and reason continued on and was at the root of the Reformation, which challenged the Church in many things that were being done in the name of faith, and this brought on the Council of Trent.

By the eighteenth century, reason was reigning supreme. This meant that those philosophers at the time were discarding much of Christian truth that could not be fathomed by human reason. There now ensued the long and bitter struggle between the great worshipers of reason and the Fathers of the Church, ending later in the First Vatican Council. As this struggle continued, more and more folks were discarding the faith dimension of their lives because it did not make any sense to them.

As the church began to listen, she was able to come to grips with a variety of issues that had been raised by the

9

people from the scientific community, applying her own wealth of information and thought accumulated over the centuries from such great minds as Augustine in the fifth century, Thomas Aquinas, Bonaventure, and others in the thirteenth and fourteenth centuries.

The crushing blow that brought the unity of Western Christianity to a sad end was, of course, the Protestant Revolution. This began as a theological debate over the interpretation of the letters of St. Paul, especially regarding the meaning of faith and salvation. The little German principalities saw this, however, as an opportunity to unshackle themselves from the power of the Holy Roman Empire, which at the time was a powerful political ally of the church. The issue now becomes a political one as well as one of reason, both now pitted against the faith as understood by the church for fifteen hundred years.

For the next four hundred years, rationalism becomes the dominant way of perceiving reality. It is known as the scientific approach. Reality is perceived only through the senses, what we can see, hear, smell, taste or touch. If it can't be weighed, measured, or counted in the laboratory, then it doesn't exist. Rationalism has perdured into our own time. There was a good side to this approach, however. Now believers have a more reasoned approach to faith. We saw that in the philosophy of both Augustine and Thomas Aquinas, each of whom developed proofs through a reasoning process for the existence of God. In this way the church was able to attract some of the best minds of the time to examine the various approaches to faith. The Oxford Movement of the late nineteenth and early twentieth century brought many noted converts to Rome, such as John Henry Newman, G. K. Chesterton, Robert Hugh Benson, and Ronald Knox.

In the early development of this movement, they were called "tractarians" because they had published a series of essays challenging some of the theology and practices of the state religion.

The same movement was taking place in the United States as a number of apologists (the name given them in this country) emerged here to carry forth the work of their brothers in England. Among these were Frank Sheed with his wife, Mazie Ward, both of whom wrote extensively in support of the Catholic Church. Eventually, they founded the well-known publishing establishment, "Sheed & Ward." This became the source for a wide variety of Catholic works in philosophy and theology as well as apologetics and scripture. Isaac Hecker was another convert of this time, the founder of the Paulist Fathers whose mission was to evangelize protestant America. As it turned out, the science and reason became partners in these apologetic movements.

Eventually, all of that was going to change. A new enemy was pounding at the gates! Midway through the twentieth century, a new way of perceiving reality was creeping into the cultural life of the Western World. Spawned by the Vietnam War and the Sexual Revolution, young Americans were abandoning the traditions and institutions of the past, creating a new world based on feeling or passion. No longer was it a question of making sense, rather does it make me feel good. And this continues to dominate the culture today, which would suggest a return to more primitive responses to reality.

The great issues we face today, as Americans and as Christians, have arisen out of this does-it-feel-good mentality: abortion, drugs, sex, euthanasia, domestic abuse, etc., etc. All such things were seen as solutions to more basic problems of life. These solutions, however, were based on sentimentality instead of reason; on what is good for me, not what is good for the community.

What has all this to do with "doublespeak," you

ask? A lot! Doublespeak is a literary tool that uses ambiguous language to straddle the gulf between reason and feeling. It is a way of using language that will make the man of reason think you are talking to him, and the person of feeling sense that you are talking to her. That you see, if you are a politician, ends up getting you two votes instead of one. That is a very simplistic way of describing it, but that really is what is going on. If one is going to win a public office, then he needs a majority of votes from the concerned constituency. He realizes that the majority do not share his thoughts or feelings about the issues, but then he has to make them all think that he does share their viewpoints. That is when the spin-doctors are invited in.

The fourth estate, i.e., the media, is not very useful either, as it tends to be less objective in the dissemination of news, and more self-serving in the way political news is presented. There is a broad assumption that all Democrats are liberal or progressive and all Republicans are conservative, which simply is not the case any more. There are wide ranges of political ideology in both parties today, and because of this variety, a new term is introduced into the political arena, namely the word "moderate." What that really means is that the moderate candidate does not want to be identified with either extreme of the party, and by assuming such a position is further blurring what the party really stands for.

The English language, at least as it occurs in these United States, has become a giant puzzle that those of my generation find difficult to unravel. The social dialog is overrun with slang, lingo, jargon, and "double speak," making it next to impossible to discern what is really being said. I recently found this verse by an anonymous author:

"We're improving immensely;

we don't steal anymore, we lift;
we don't lie anymore, we misinform;
we don't fornicate, we only fool around;
we don't kill, we terminate a pregnancy."

This problem emerges in some of the published literature of the day. Speed reading or scanning is impossible in trying to find the sense or meaning of the language used in these. I fear that I may also be using such language, hopefully though, in a context that will give a clearer meaning to any such buzz words of the day, that even I might employ. We now explore some of the obstacles we are facing as we pursue this road to human wholeness.

REFLECTION I

AN UNCERTAIN FUTURE

It would seem that the underlying cause of all of the social and moral evils of our time is rooted in the loss of manhood. Manhood, fatherhood, masculinity - however you want to put it. This important aspect of human existence has been relegated to the secular city's garbage dump. Until we find a way of retrieving that principle, things can only get worse. We live in a society devoid of its fathers - of its fathering energy. With all of the push of the feminist agenda, we have to ask ourselves, are we any better off today than we were twenty-five years ago? The statistics will certainly verify it, when I say we are far worse off - not because of the presence of women in so many aspects of society today - but because of the absence of real men - real maleness - real fatherhood.

That is what I want to reflect on in the pages that follow. How can we reclaim that principle in our own lives, in the life of our families, in the church, as well as in the general social order - the principle which we call "masculine spirituality?"

It is an overwhelming challenge to be certain. But, I am convinced that we must vigorously pursue this challenge, if we are to resolve the enormous problems that confront humanity today. Mine is not to present a scientific examination of this issue, but rather to present reflections on the cultural scene as I have experienced it for eighty-five years. This will be an attempt to ask the right questions; to stimulate further reflection and discussion; and to suggest some possible avenues of remedy or therapy.

I will endeavor to weave together insights that I have come to from a lot of my experiences of the last few years. In prayer and serious reflection, I have tried to relate Jungian depth psychology, twelve step programs, biblical anthropology, the Meyers-Briggs TI and the Enneagram personality typology, with the hope that we can come to some understanding of the deep roots of the problems we face in our society today. Each chapter will treat a different aspect of what it means to be a man, or a woman, in the world God has created, and how that has all been distorted in a world heavily covered by secular humanism, psychological humanism, materialism, and hedonism.

THE INSIGHT OF HENRI NOUWEN

Some years ago, (1969 to be exact) in response to the challenge of the Second Vatican Council, the University of Notre Dame sponsored a workshop entitled, "The Church of Tomorrow." I was fortunate to be able to attend this very challenging workshop. Notre Dame had gathered prestigious scholars in a variety of academic disciplines, each of whom presented a paper addressing the question: "What will the Church look like by the new millennium?"

Among those invited was Father Henri Nouwen, a Dutch theologian at the time on the faculty of Notre Dame. He spoke to the topic, "Christian Leadership of Tomorrow." In his paper he suggested that there would be three qualities to characterize the people of tomorrow, the men and women we would be ministering to and with, at the end of the century. He addressed these comments from the point of view of pastoral theology. By looking at his own experience of people at that time, he projected into the future what he considered to be the results that he had observed in his ministry. He singled out the three qualities that would characterize the children of tomorrow. Thirty years later, at the dawn of the new millennium, we have to agree that Henri Nouwen was right on target. The qualities he projected were: inwardness, fatherlessness, and convulsiveness.

Inwardness, for example, is best demonstrated by the frightening growth of "new age" programs, activities, and literature that seemed to mushroom in the 1970's and 1980's - all pointing inward. Many, many people were giving up on the world around to find comfort and solace in the world within. The only god in that world is the "self." In such a world there is no room for a Christian God or any external deity.

Fatherlessness - the absence of father is a common experience in all too many American homes today. Mothers are raising children by themselves either because of divorce, abandonment, or they simply choose to mother fatherless children. The statistics on the breakup of the traditional family is very discouraging for those who see family life as a foundational value for any real culture.

Before we go into other issues let me say, by way of repetition, a few more things about the absent father syndrome. When we speak about the absent father, we are not just talking about homes where the single parent is the mother. We are talking about families where the father may be physically absent for other reasons than divorce; he may be on the road a good deal, perhaps as a salesman, or a service worker; he may be in the military; he may be spending long hours at work; or he may be even too involved in outside activities in the church or other civic good works. Whatever takes him out of the home and away from the family, at times when he really should be a part of their lives, he is an absent father.

The father can be absent emotionally or psychologically as well. The stress and tension of the work place brings him home totally exhausted. His preference then is to abandon himself to total passivity with the aid of the TV. He does not want to deal with the tensions and stresses of the family.

The reason why the father is absent doesn't make any difference to the young boy or girl. His or her experience will be the same: rejection, abandonment, and worthlessness. The child feels that he is not worth much when his father can't be present to him, or that there is something wrong with himself. He does not perceive at all that the problem is with the father. This begins to generate, within the soul of the young male, those ambivalent feelings toward the father that we mentioned elsewhere: a deep sense of resentment and anger because the father was not there when he needed him; and his ongoing drive or urge to find that father's love and affirmation, so that he can fulfill or complete his own growth process toward manhood.

In his insightful book, James L. Schaller writes about "orphan psychology," an experience any boy or girl will have when they are deprived of authentic fathering. He states, *"some fathers deplete rather than give. A father who beats, molests, verbally degrades, or disrupts the stability of the home by his alcohol, drugs or moodiness, is an anti-father. He sucks the life from the veins of his family, he functions as an emotional black hole. He steals the carefree laughter of childhood. Such a father produces a large amount of psychic orphanhood in his children forcing them to function as emotional orphans, even though both parents are still alive."*[2]

Thirdly, convulsiveness, which is exemplified by all of the erratic and undisciplined behavior we see all

---

2   The Search for Lost Fathering, James L. Schaller, p.65

over today: drugs, violence, sex, domestic abuse, suicide and arson. All of this was magnified enormously by what has happened to the world since September 11, 2001. The situation in the middle east is a remarkable example of what happens when everyone does "his own thing."

Even in the face of the evidence, all three of these characteristics are in a general state of denial in most societies today, and our churches have been swept along as well. One of the big problems Christianity faces today is the fact that the average in-pew parishioner, in any middle class church, does not want to hear the gospel preached in a way where one has to confront evil, especially the evil present in their own lives. They only want to hear things that are pleasant and comforting. "After all, isn't that why we go to church - to be uplifted, to be encouraged," which really means to be lulled into apathy and complacency. If that is the common and universal attitude among Christians and is tolerated by those who preach, the result is that we develop what psychologists call a "state of denial." Denial is an attitude or defense mechanism that people assume so they don't have to deal with a difficult issue. There is a wonderful example of this in the film, "The Prince of Tides." In this story the family pretends that a horrible trauma that they experienced doesn't exist, or didn't happen. And they keep telling themselves that over and over, until they soon began to believe it and act as though the trauma never occurred.

We know from counseling (and the movie brings it out) that the only way to deal with a difficult problem or situation, be it something personal, relational, or social, is to confront it and resolve it. If we do not do that, the issue doesn't go away by ignoring it, suppressing it, or denying it. It hangs around and becomes a destructive influence in our lives.

These reflections that I have put together will be dealing with a cultural denial phenomenon that has enveloped the society in which we live and the church in which we seek salvation. The culture of the "first world," particularly the western world, might be viewed as profoundly ill. Of course, we do not want to admit it, and so we don't. There are a lot of things amiss in the society in which we live, which we continue to ignore, deny, or repress. What we tend to grapple with are the symptoms; we don't seem to have the wisdom, or perhaps the courage - the manly energy - to deal with the underlying causes. As a culture we prefer to live in a state of denial!

Two examples of recent history seem to exemplify what I am saying here: the Iraq war, and the sexual scandal in the Catholic Church. It would appear that we have neither the will nor the wisdom to get a handle on these two difficult problems. Perhaps by looking at the issues, suggested here in depth, more light can be shown on these events as well. Maybe we will learn that it takes more manly courage to practice diplomacy than to wage war; to get at the roots of a problem than to apply band-aids to the symptoms.

THE CLOUDY PRESENT

In the beginning of the human experience culture and religious faith were indistinguishable. With the advent of revealed religion, a rift begins to emerge. Little by little culture and society became inimical to the values that revealed religion espoused. The periods of that history, in which culture and religion mutually influenced each other, were very few indeed. That has been particularly true of Christianity during its 2000 year history. The cultural situation of today, which is described here, isn't something new. Because of the amazing advances in modern technology, however, its influence is far greater today than ever before.

Over and over again, the principle of evil seems to be able to set the rules for the game of life. What was described in the third chapter of the book of Genesis is played out in society in each era of human existence. This evil influence, or anti-God influence, seems to have as its goal, the creation of a totally secular society. Looking at what is going on from our own modern perspective, it would seem there is an orderly pattern to it all. As I see it, there are six steps or levels in the plan:

First, eliminate faith in a supreme being. Do not believe in, trust in, or submit to a God who is understood to be the supreme author of all that is, the ultimate authority, and the great provider. That was precisely what Satan achieved in the story of the Fall, sowing doubts in the heart of Eve about God, who had given the rules. The temptation was a suggestion for her to take charge and control over her own life, to be as gods. Listen to Satan: *". . you certainly will not die! No, God knows well that the moment you eat of it your eyes will be opened and you will be like gods who know what is good and what is bad." (Gen. 3:4)* We know what happened as a result. This story may or may not have any historical value, but it does describe with great accuracy what seems to have occurred in the primordial human experience.

Once Eve shook off the sensed shackles of divine order, she and her progeny took on the shackles of secular servitude instead. We human beings were made to know, love, and serve a God. If we do not serve Jahweh, we will create our own gods to serve. The history of humanity is a history of searching for gods that will suit our whims and desires. All of our turbulent history is a record of moving from one god to another, always looking for those gods that will serve us, rather than we serving them. The Old

Testament history of Israel is a rebellious search for other gods, that would satisfy their needs and not make such burdensome demands on them. That would follow, of course, with repentance and return to Jahweh. Over and over that scenario would be played out throughout their turbulent history.

In step two, we divest ourselves of our very spirituality, an integral part of our human nature. If there be no God out there, then there is no God in here either. The whole spiritual order comes under attack once we deny the existence of the biblical God. We then live as though there is nothing other than this world and that it is the totality of being. In denying our own spirituality, and the vast reaches of the spiritual order that exists out there, we cripple ourselves, and condemn ourselves to an existence that is devalued, deformed, and purposeless.

This next step now attacks the whole question of authority. The word "authority" normally conjures up the persons or institutions that make the rules and enforces them. We think of God and the Ten Commandments with the sanction of eternal damnation for non-compliance; we think of the government with its laws and penalties; we think of institutions, like our schools and colleges with their sanctions for non-observance as well; and we think of the Church with its structures of authority. All these we perceive, in our new found freedom from God, as being oppressive and restrictive and in violation of our basic human goals or "rights," which is the buzz word of the day. We find ourselves confronting all these authority aspects of our lives. One by one we divest ourselves of them, seeking that great freedom for which we yearn. The result of all this process is what the secular city is really like: chaos, anarchy, and incredible violence. As I was writing these lines, the news of the massacre at Virginia Tech broke in upon my consciousness, one more awful example of what happens in the secular city.

In step four, we easily eliminate all moral directives. If there be no God, no spirituality, and no authority, then why should we be shackled by all these moral derivatives - the shalls and the shall nots. If there be no God in charge, if he does not make the rules, then we are free now, to do as we decide and choose. What is moral is whatever is good for me, whatever delights and gives me value and pleasure. I am the ultimate foundation of my choices and decisions. No law, no rule, no person, no institution can tell me what I should or should not do.

The next thing that is destroyed in this secularization process is Christian sexuality. If there be no God, no spirituality, no authority, or no morality, then we are perfectly free to make sex our god. Our society is obsessed with sex and nowhere is this more evident than in the media. All aspects of social communication are obsessed with sex. The more perverse, the more bizarre, and the more ugly sexual behavior, the more the media loves to inflict us with it. Without God in charge, without knowing our own spiritual nature, without morality and authority, where do we get the guidance and direction in our sexual living? Ourselves, of course! And that is what we have done - focus on our own personal desires and urges. We have turned what was a survival or life goal into a pleasure or self-gratification goal. Listen to the rhetoric of those who promote sex as a pleasure commodity, and you will pick up the message that the life-value of sexuality is considered a misfortune, an accident, or even a disease. In the whole dialog surrounding the abortion issue, the message that comes through from the "pro choice" folks is the idea that to be "pregnant" for some is akin to a sexually transmitted disease. Everyone has the right to sex of any kind, with anyone, as long as it is fun. What ever happened to discipline? That also went out with authority. What ever happened to self-control? That is medieval! What ever happened to the sanctity of life, the thrill of new life? That went out with spirituality. And the questions go on. The god of modern men and women of freedom is sex or pleasure. But that is the god that has destroyed commitment, responsibility, family values, and the family itself. Could we then be on the brink of human annihilation?

The last phase of the downward spiral of our secular society is the devaluing of life itself. Our society, in the last two generations, has turned itself completely around in regard to life. We have become a society with a death wish. Our focus is on death, particularly death as a solution to the difficulties of life. Is this not true in the abortion question? Unfortunately, that is only the beginning, because we are discovering that death is becoming the solution to other social problems - euthanasia, Kevorkian suicide, and throw away babies. How soon will we be eliminating other undesirable persons in our society simply by "putting them to sleep?" We stand in hypocritical awe before the Jewish Holocaust of the German Nazi state, but we never talk about the millions of German citizens that were gassed simply because they were perceived as being useless in the Third Reich: the retarded, the insane, the feeble, the senile, and the crippled. Is that not what some folks are about in our society today, purifying society, playing God with people's lives and destinies; making decisions about life and death that only God can make? On the other hand, others are doing great things to improve the quality of life.

That is the world in which we are called to live. We cannot escape. This secularism is so pervasive that it finds itself impregnated in the very fabric of our lives, and this unfortunately, includes the Church as well. We have been evangelized much more by the culture than we have by the Gospel. And yet, isn't that what Christianity should be about, constantly challenging the prevailing mores and ethics and offering real salvation to the peoples of the earth? To do this we need to retrieve our lost heritage of deep faith in God, and with that faith see the importance and value of our spiritual nature in regard to such things as authority, morality, and wholesome sexuality, as well as a deep respect for the value and dignity of all life wherever we find it.

REFLECTION II

ORIGINS OF THE PROBLEM

In this chapter we will consider the roots of the problem of vanishing manhood as it appears to have developed here in the United States. How did we get into this situation? Where are its origins, its roots? To understand, in any depth at all, why we are where we are today, requires but a quick recall of the European Philosophies of the eighteenth and nineteenth centuries. Factors that have played an influential role in our American culture are deeply rooted in these philosophies that were imported from Europe: pragmatism, secularism, and egalitarianism, each of which you can discern in the Declaration of Independence and in the United States Constitution with its Bill of Rights. How were these philosophies interpreted by the American experience, and what were the factors derived from them that have so influenced our nation building? The historical or sociological events or movements that began the process of male disintegration will be our focus as we move ahead in this chapter. The most significant events as I see them were: 1. The American Revolution; 2. The Industrial Revolution; and 3. The Educational Revolution.

Each one of these movements have, in one way or another, contributed immeasurably to the growth and welfare of our country. Yet, each of them also possessed its own dark side.

THE AMERICAN REVOLUTION

I begin with this 1776 event because it has become a significant turning point in how men perceived themselves. Pre-revolutionary America, or Colonial America, as I shall call it here, gave us a picture of male life and family life much different from what we experience today. Without question, Colonial America was a patriarchal society. That social construct came with the early settlers as they migrated from their European lands. These men had very little similarity to the males of modern America. The colonial world they created was a man's world. These men were courageous, inventive, persevering, and attentive to the needs of their wives and children.

By researching historical accounts of colonial life, one discovers a different kind of manhood than we have today. Men in that historic time were very much in charge of all of life. They ruled their homes, they dominated public and social life, and they were much involved in all spiritual matters. It appears that the Colonial father would be expected to rise to leadership in these areas. Politics and religion were dominant themes of discussion in any gathering of men at the time. Unlike too many men today, who regularly abdicate all religious responsibilities to their wives, Colonial men took this onus very seriously, not only in their homes, but in the various church communities where they regularly worshiped. It was noted somewhere that the most frequent worshipers in these Colonial churches were the men.

Where did the women fit into this scene? I'm quite certain that the feminine counterparts of today would likely gasp in horror at the life style of these eighteenth century women. But do they really need to be pitied? Perhaps envy would be a better reaction. Colonial women didn't seem to suffer from some of the common problems and illnesses afflicting the ladies of the present. Why? Life was simpler, of course, and they were generally treated very well by the men in their lives. Men knew who they were as men, and they had great respect for the women in their lives. Where real manhood is lived out in a community, women tend to be more productive and happier.

As an aside here, in Colonial American life, the settlers generally enjoyed good relationships with the native peoples, because they were willing to accept the fact that they were visitors, and they needed to negotiate for whatever they might require from the resources of the Indians, and pay for them in kind. That attitude will end with the changes that took place after the Revolutionary War.

As the burdens of the rule and the taxation of the British monarchy became more and more oppressive, the colonists began a search for relief, and retaliated with violent responses to this oppression. This provoked the English to transport legions of British soldiers to bring order and compliance in the colonies. Little by little the men of the colonies began to organize themselves as they saw the necessity of creating their own army to withstand the advances of the British troops.

This finally led to the "Declaration of Independence." This manifesto was not universally accepted by the colonists, many of them remaining loyal to the Crown. This document of rebellion set the stage for the Revolutionary War. Eventually, the colonists were able to overcome the English guns and bayonets and achieve a shaky victory. Independence was purchased at a great cost: an incredible number of lives sacrificed in behalf of the cause; in the loss of many assets rendering this new nation bankrupt; in the devastation of many farms; and the destruction of great portions of the larger municipalities.

The Revolution was born out of an admirable desire to shrug off oppressive British rule, and as so often happens, "the baby gets thrown out with the bath water." In this case the baby was that essential paternal impulse of colonial life. Instead of correctly identifying and rebelling against an oppressive patriarchy, these new Americans began to look upon all patriarchy as inherently evil, and became intent on being ruled by no one. We will see this in the ofttimes turbulent wrangling that took place both in the creation of the Declaration of Independence and the United States Constitution. The spirit of independence soon began to permeate every aspect of American life. Yes, independence and individualism began to be viewed as national virtues. As history began to unfold here, these values found themselves infiltrating all of society: the homes, the churches, and the schools. This social aspect of the revolution had a profound effect on the way men perceived their own manhood.

Men now felt they needed to tame this wild and vast land, and help build up the new republic. The consequence of this determination was his disengagement from his community, his church, and too often even his family. Many of these now freed and independent males began to move west. They did not realize how vast this new area was and all of the various Native tribes there were, some of whom had been removed from the original thirteen colonies. Now, instead of bargaining and negotiating with the native peoples, these new adventurers simply took them over, at the cost of many native lives. From then on, it was this type of white man they would have to contend with. These pioneers were generally successful as they often had the backing of the U.S. Army. Looking at this change from a psychological level, we see the "warrior" archetype mutated into a "pirate" archetype.

On the faith level, self-ordained preacher types, missioned by no one, with the Bible tucked under their arms, mounted their horses and were off to minister to the wondering frontiersman, and to Christianize the native populations. These were the kind of men, both the adventurers and preachers, that the native populations had to deal with. Many of these traveling preachers, alive with the spirit of independence, began to establish independent churches, leading to the further fracturing of an already divided Christianity.

It was these wild frontiersmen types that began creating the problems with the native peoples. To prove to themselves, as much as to others, that they were real men, they began taking over the lands of others, even molesting them or killing them. There was no recognition of prior ownership or the need to negotiate and compromise. They just took.

The magnitude of this shift, from a caring, supporting patriarchal society to one in which each person was his own authority, had devastating consequences on the social, economic, political, and religious fabric of this new nation - consequences whose evils we are living with today.

THE INDUSTRIAL REVOLUTION

The second momentous change, that has contributed to the disintegration of the family and the emasculation of the male, was the industrial revolution. Prior to the great inventions of the nineteenth century, the primary cultural context in which men raised their families was agrarian. They worked the land and were supported by the land. Yes, there were service businesses, but these were generally run by families, where the members worked side by side. Prior to this revolution, boys lived in the shadow of their fathers, they were with him most of the day; they absorbed his values and his attitudes, his way of dealing with life, even his mannerisms, and his psychic energy. They knew from their observation and experience of their fathers what it meant to be a man, to be a male, to be a husband, to be a father, and to be a leader. Granted there were some unholy exceptions to all of this, but the basic cultural context was quite healthy.

With the development of the industrial revolution, people moved off the farms and land and went to the cities to work in the mines, the factories, and the shops. Men were taken out of the home at an early hour of the day and returned only late at night, many times even seven days a week. Children rarely saw their fathers! Consequently, the mother was forced to assume much of the father's role in rearing the children. No longer did boys have the privilege and grace of being in their father's shadow.

As generation followed generation, the young men were becoming less and less men, not that they were effeminate, but their maleness became warped. They developed more out of the expectations of mother or society, rather than by the example of "live-in" fathers. As a result, another image also emerges - the "macho" type. Boys began to perceive manhood in this model, which was a pretty negative perception of maleness, lacking, as it did, sensitivity, commitment, and spirituality. Along side of this was another more feminine image lacking the qualities of aggression, spontaneity, and creativity. This youngster could never quite see that he really belonged between these two extremes, a middle ground as it were, or the traditional image, because there was no father around to pass it on.

Now eight generations later, we are reaping the fruits of this second level of emasculation. Boys and girls both need their fathers for appropriate gender identification.

Mothers give their children identity as persons, as a human being; but only the father (or father surrogate) can give them their identity as a man or as a woman. This surely is one of the functions of true father energy. For the most part, all too many people today are growing up lacking this identity. Most of the turmoil and upheaval we see in youth culture is directly related to this identity crisis. Both young men, and today more and more young women, are seeking that identity, desperately searching for someone who will say: "You are man; You are woman."

In more recent times, men may not be in the factories and mines; but they are on the road (or in the air) as salesmen, or in the white collar factories of corporate business and government service. These men, too often, are in bondage to the corporation they work for, and too often, in order to move up and get ahead in the rat race, they spend many hours at their jobs, hours that should be spent at home with their families. I recently heard a statistic showing that the forty hour week is a thing of the past.

Other fathers, who may have time at home are often emotionally unavailable. They are not comfortable with the world of feelings and domestic problems. They come home exhausted from the tensions and stresses of the job, feel they do not need any more tension or stress, and so collapse into a world of passivity. The child then has no opportunity to develop a warm relationship with his or her father. We can see then, how in our culture there emerges a vast number of what I call "psychic orphans."

In his book, "The Search for Lost Fathering", James Schaller devotes an entire chapter to "Orphan Psychology"[3] in which he observes that most children will experience orphan emotions, even when both parents are,

_____
3   The Search for Lost Fathering by James L. Schaller, pp.64-5

in fact, living. When father and/or mother are unavailable, because of their own commitments, the child will feel left out, abandoned, and alone. This is the feeling of the orphan. In ancient cultures, very often when the father died, the children were called orphans, which recognizes the importance of the role he plays in a child's development.

Too often, what occurs is that mom and dad provide a house and the physical necessities of life, but they are too busy with their own things to truly be father and mother to these children, a full time job in itself.

AMERICAN PUBLIC EDUCATION

Another moment of downgrading the American male occurs when he enters the public school system. I am quite aware that when one starts talking about public education he may be treading on dangerous grounds. It is not so much public education that is being challenged here, rather the philosophical and psychological underpinnings of that system, which gives public education, and even most sectarian educational systems their purpose and goal.

As I run a critical eye over public education, know likewise, I do not intend in any way to pass judgment on individual teachers or administrators involved in the system. They are as much victimized by the system as the students. We all know truly magnificent men and women, who have been both teachers and administrators, that have battled these tendencies in heroic ways, and made a contribution to a better vision of what real education could and ought to be.

The beginnings of education in America were rooted in the strong religious schools that were part of the cultural heritage that came over from Europe during the early migrations. Most of them were Protestant. The prestigious universities of the Ivy League were all strong religious schools in the beginning, many of them founded to educate the clergy. Some continue to maintain their religious character to this day.

In the middle of the nineteenth century, a visionary by the name of Horace Mann, began an effort to democratize education in America. He is seen by many as the father of American public education. His dream, a worthy one indeed, was to have every citizen of this vast country given the opportunity for an education. Prior to this time, many citizens were deprived of such an opportunity for a number of reasons: either they could not afford it; it was too far to travel; or they were needed to work the family farm or business.

Good ideas often times also have an unforeseen dark side. In the case of Horace Mann's dream, as it began to unfold in America and as it developed, the side effects began to emerge as well. "Everyone should have the opportunity to learn to read and write in order to become productive members of society," was the theme of the movement.

Recall that education up to that time had been masculine oriented; it had a strong left brain approach; it was primarily for men. It was based on the assumption that only men needed an education. At the time it seemingly did not occur, to either Horace Mann or his followers, that there was a serious need to change the style and the content of education that had been offered in the sectarian schools (not its religious content, but its heavily rational content). The advocates of Horace Mann's system simply took over the curriculum of these schools, minus the religious content. Their goal was to make education available to all. For the first several generations of educators, the ethic, the morality, and even the doctrine of mainline Protestantism was effectively carried into the public schools. This, no doubt, was a factor that forced the growing Roman Catholic Church to establish its own parochial school system.

One can see how complicated this will eventually become as the years move on. Let us return to our consideration of the side effects of Horace Mann's dream. As universal education was gradually implemented throughout the country, and as everyone was more or less required to go to school, all were exposed to the only education available, which was strongly protestant in spirit, left brain in its approach, and pragmatic. The idea was to assist the citizen to enter the world of politics, business, and the professions.

For one hundred and fifty years women were entering a public educational process to be evangelized by protestant ideals, masculine rationalism, and pragmatism, not to mention what we have already considered, namely, independence and rugged individualism. In its wake, this educational construct will eventually be destructive of genuine femininity as well.

On the other hand, the system as it developed, also turned out to be detrimental to the boys. Let me suggest the reason. To implement his dream, Horace Mann needed a lot of teachers. Men were very busy exploring the frontier and building the nation. They were not that interested in teaching, particularly children. Consequently, Mann needed to turn to women for his teachers; these ladies then created their version of school, a feminine world into which little boys were brought anticipating that they would turn into educated men. This was not to happen, however. For over a century young boys have been entering the public school system with startling disadvantages. From the very onset, the educational deck is stacked against them. The vast majority of elementary public school teachers were women. That would work fine for the girls, who are ready to be schooled in a feminine environment, where they sit quietly, listen to the teacher, and take notes with their newly acquired skills in penmanship. Reading stories and gaining facts from books come easily for girls. They are usually eager to repeat the assignments they have been asked to memorize.

Boys, on the other hand, are quickly bored with this seemingly passive style of schooling; they have little interest in sitting still and being quiet. Reading and memorizing do not fit into the real world of young males. No matter how many words pass through the air, being seated in one place for long periods of time does not connect with the natural processes by which boys learn. Most boys intuitively know that. Those first years in elementary school come at a time when a boy is developing inherent masculine tendencies. He is shaping his skills for courage and strength. Thus he is constantly seeking action. While girls tend to want to think and feel, boys would rather see and do. They want to participate with vigorous verbal contact and aggressive physical action. The perfectly normal actions that boys display do not evoke approval of a female dominated system, even on the school playground. What is natural to young males is often viewed as bad behavior. Many normal boys are labeled "bad boys" early in life, when they are simply trying to discover their masculinity through innocent episodes of competitive game playing.   Christina Hoff Summers, the mother of two boys, challenges the feminist assertion that girls are short changed in our schools, a big issue in the early 1990's. In her book, "The War Against Boys," she collects honest data and reputable statistics to demonstrate that it is boys, not girls, who are on the short end of the educational process.

America's school boys are troubled. From the very onset of their educational experience, they are subjected to a host of feminizing forces that create a sometimes unresolvable tug-of-war between being "good" and being "male." They are forced into making a choice they should never have to make. We will have more to say about this when we examine the basic qualities of maleness. The Roman Catholic Church may have been wise in its educational approach in the last century by educating boys and girls separately.

Since World War II, American education, both public and religious has been universally influenced by a philosophy of education which is called "Progressive Education." Founded primarily by a man, John Dewey, a professor at Columbia University, whose system based on three assumptions, has succeeded in completely revolutionizing American education.

Socialism. The human person is a social animal and should imbibe attitudes and behavior that promotes social values and social living. Previous education, these folks would observe, was too individualistic with its emphasis on excellence, literacy, and traditional values.

Humanism. With an emphasis on the value of man (the human person) in himself or herself, there is no need to emphasize such theological concepts as God, salvation, or eternal life. . . and certainly not sin, hell, or the devil. Man is for all intents and purposes in the view of these progressives an end in himself. We observe here that the New Age phenomenon that emerged during the 1970's an 1980's is indebted to this philosophy.

Behaviorism. This psychological theory looks upon the human being as nothing more than a mechanical animal; all behavior is absolutely predictable. If you teach them the right things, they will respond in an appropriate way. There is no recognition in the behavioral school for divine grace or free will. Everything is perceived in stimuli/response categories.

These assumptions have conspired to form a populace today in America, that generally has no practical belief in God; has completely abandoned most traditional values; and has dedicated their lives to consumerism and hedonism.

Through the influence of progressive education, our culture today has moved away from a people that held values and relationships as very important to the maintenance and development of culture, to a people that looks upon things and pleasure (self-gratification) as the real values. The sexual revolution, the drug addiction, and all the violence we see, may well be seen as an outcome of this kind of life philosophy. It all boils down to "do your own thing, if it makes you feel good." What began as an attack on individualism has, in fact, made it worse. The monster they sought to destroy has only grown larger. No place on earth, or in history, have human beings been so individualistic, so self-centered, or isolated from one another as they are today. We see this in the trend to build larger and larger homes on larger and larger lots, even acres. The most recent communication tools now on the market will only further isolate us from one another. The entire world has been contaminated by these side effects.

The big question now is: how does all of this contribute to fatherlessness in our society? One of the qualities of authentic manhood is the ability to be disciplined, and once having learned discipline, is able to take charge of others. Discipline means to make disciples by teaching, by leading, and by example. In a society focused so much on doing one's own thing, men are not likely to be disciplined, nor would such men be able to discipline others. "You cannot give what you do not have!" We generally experience this in politics and economics today.

We find most people today terribly undisciplined; there is no aspect of their concupiscence that they are able to control, nor even the desire to do so. They drink too much, they eat too much, they talk too much, they fight too much, et al. This is the convulsiveness that Henri Nouwen spoke about in his paper, "the Church of Tomorrow," which I referred to earlier. There are other values that disappeared with fathering as well: responsibility, accountability, obedience, and authority. How can society function without these?

We live in a world today, in a culture populated by males, who have not been energized by appropriate father energy for the simple reason that society forbids discipline. There is no room for father in today's world. For some of our die-hard feminists this seems to be an ideal to be sought. Margaret Mead, a well-known anthropologist, suggests that man's role in the world might be unnecessary. Another source suggests that maleness is even abnormal or a genetic mutation of some kind. Attend to what is being said here! Maleness is abnormal, undesirable, an accidental mutation, resulting in no good for the race. It is not the irresponsibility of manhood that is being attacked here, but maleness itself is under attack. I read another book, one of the bibles of the feminist movement, in which this is the dominant theme that the author explores and promotes.

The most tragic thing about this warped view of maleness is that even some men believe it. This, in turn, leads to some very bizarre consequences. The sad truth may well be that there is no room for mother either, and that's the message from our abortion activists. Too many women do not want to be mothers, and even when they do give birth to a child, they do not want to mother that child, which is another side effect of what we have been talking about. Having children and raising children is mighty inconvenient, with an investment of a good deal of time, struggle, and a lot of pain. Who needs that in a culture that canonizes pleasure?

A final question now: "Does this have anything to do with church? It doesn't take a lot of reflection to see how these attitudes and philosophies that we have been writing about have made serious inroads into the church – all churches. The values that have formed us in our modern cultural situation also find their way eventually into the church world. Often they are disguised in nice sounding theological or ecclesiastical language, but "the wolf disguised in sheep's clothing is still a wolf." All the confusion, and negativism that we see in our churches today comes from the philosophies we have been looking at here. No one wants to be told what to do! Not even the most conservative among us. No one wants to submit to any discipline; few indeed are they who are able to offer discipline, and those who do, probably should not, because they do it out of their own need to control or promote themselves. Both the extremists from the left and from the right are operating from values that find their roots in the philosophy of progressive education. These ideas have found their way into all aspects of our lives, and in all the institutions we rely on for assistance in the world of today: economics, politics, military, athletics, banking, communications, and yes, religion. For example, televangelism took a big hit in the 1970's and 1980's with the exposure of scandals surrounding the ministries of Jim Jones, Jim Bakker, and Jim Swaggart. In each case, success was not handled with humility. And each, in turn, were overcome by those three evil titans – greed, lust, pride. Now in these early years of the twenty-first century, my own church has been devastated by a series of sexual crimes involving our clergy, who also gave in to those evil spirits of lust, pride, and greed. In all of these situations God, while not condoning the behavior, at the same time can bring good out of it, by purifying and renewing the ministers who have been called to serve him.

In review, the American male has become a conundrum today, not knowing who he is or what he is supposed to do. These three powerful social revolutions have effectively destroyed his masculine soul: the American Revolution, with its focus on independence; the Industrial Revolution, which drove him out of the family; and the Educational Revolution, that has turned his soul inside out.

REFLECTION III

OTHER RELATED ISSUES

Originally, I had planned to write this book with "fatherlessness" as my central focus. As I continued to read and reflect about this, it became more and more clear to me that at the root of that issue was this deeper suffering in society - the absence of authentic manhood. Consequently, the issues in this chapter may connect more directly to this deeper theme than to the lack of fathering.

SECULARISM

In any discussion about the life and ministry of Pope John Paul II, one continually hears comments that are tainted with secularistic values. "Oh yes, I admire this great man, but I can't accept his teachings." Why? For Americans, most of his comments had to deal with the "Culture of Death" that exists in this country including such evils as abortion, euthanasia and the death penalty. All of these issues are ways in which Americans generally respond to certain inconveniences in their lives. If it is inconvenient, then kill it, it seems to say.

Again, we ask why? There are many factors involved here, but we will endeavor to bring out the more important ones in this reflection. The very first reality we have to face is the fact that most Americans do not live from their heads; they do not live by principle or rule. They live out of their feelings or hormones. Again why?

Because we have adopted the religion of secularism – this says that there is nothing besides this world, which leads to the conclusion that man, the human being is, in fact, the center of the universe and his own god.

In America and in western civilization generally, there is little or no belief in God. We are not people of faith. Faith issues, faith values do not influence our lives all that much. Worse yet is that fact that values based on reason, or logic, or principle no longer influence the way we live either.

The problem with all of this is that we have no guide posts, no starting points, no beacons to guide our thinking, or our behavior in the world. We are living in a time of moral anarchy, and we have seen how this has gradually infiltrated other aspects of culture, for we can see the anarchy now prevalent in politics, in economics, and in the social order. Is this not how we see the malaise in which our federal government finds itself in at this time?

To return to the faith issue and the teachings of the church, John Paul or any Pope, at least in the last century, did not create any new teachings or doctrines. What they did was reiterate the ancient truths that have guided the church for hundreds of years. These principles are derived from an in-depth study of the Sacred Scriptures, and the traditions of the early church. In each generation, the Pope, whoever he might be, will cast these principles in the language of the time, so that they can be understood by contemporary faithful.

When I was in the seminary, and in the early days of the priesthood, there were many who violated the principles, but they always recognized that the principles were important values, even though they were not living them, and humbly confessed the sinfulness of their waywardness. The call they heard was to enter the struggle to live more ethical and moral lives by searching out the means that would help them to live according to the principles of their faith.

What occurs today is that people struggle to reconstruct the whole moral teachings of Christ and his Church in a way that will fit their behavior. The Church is often accused of being out of touch with the modern world. That is a difficult accusation to prove. Obviously, such people have not been reading or listening to the statements coming forth from the Holy See, or even from our National Bishops' Conference. The church has a more honest perception of the modern world than most others, because they look at the world with a long range view. Americans look only at the moment, too often they do not consider the long term consequences of their behavior, when they reject or deny Biblical and Church teachings.

The sad reality of all of this is that the many millions of us, who claim to be Christian, or Jewish, or Islamic, have been propagandized by the prophets of secularity, and have gradually nibbled away at the principles and values that our various faith traditions have bequeathed to us.

HOMOSEXUALITY

In connection with what I have written so far, there is a need for some serious reflection on the subject of homosexuality. This is becoming an increasingly difficult issue in our country today. We surely have a need for some sane understanding regarding this condition and of the issues it is spawning. As one shall see, it is directly related to the absent father question, one of the more painful consequences of the lack of fathering.

Psychologists of the Freudian school continue to attribute the homosexual condition to a domineering mother. Perhaps not! A better examination of the issue would not suggest such a conclusion.

Recall what was said earlier about the need for same gender love in the life of a teenage boy. This love usually comes to fulfillment at the time of his physical and sexual development. As he pursues the task of personal identity vis-a-vis the physical changes taking place in his body, and the emotional changes occurring within his psyche, he needs to be loved and affirmed by his father and named "man" by him. He will not move to a true heterosexual relationship until this psychic need is met.

Facing the reality that at this moment of history there is a significant depletion of masculine energy, one can understand why the homosexual problem is so widespread. In a sense, one can say that most men today have been deprived of this basic human need. Most men, therefore, suffer from some degree of homosexuality. Because of this deficit in his psychological development, the male reaches out to other men for this masculine energy they lack. Instinct tells him that it is only from another man that he can obtain it. One sees this reaching-out occurring in many ways: the passion for athletics; the Wednesday night bowling league; the after hours experience at the local bar; the Saturday morning golf foursome; even the Friday morning prayer breakfast. There is a deep need in the heart of a man for some kind of manly support that these activities seem to supply.

However, within these very common cultural activities, there is the unconscious hope for and reaching out for the healing of that inner emptiness, that father did not supply. In the company of other males, the hope is that he can be named and be affirmed as a man and be loved by a "father."

As one may already suspect, homosexuality is a coat of many colors, many different shades and levels of need, and the behavior to meet them. I discern at this time three basic levels of homosexuality. First, there is the "homosocial" person who seeks his identity in one or more of the activities just listed. Secondly, there is the homophile person, the one who feels an attraction toward someone of the same gender because he sees in that person or persons the qualities and virtues and experiences he should have in order to be fulfilled. He wants to be loved by that person so he can absorb those energies; or he wants to embrace that energy and take it to himself. It is emotional, yes, because of the depth of the need. But at this level, there doesn't seem to be any urge to express this in a genital experience. The third level is what can be called homogenital, acting out the homosexual need through genital experience. All three levels are truly homosexual; but this third level only, is that to which the term "gay" would apply.

When people speak about homosexuality, they seem to operate under certain assumptions that they take for granted. Upon closer examination these often cannot be verified. Most of these assumptions are basically untrue and have been foisted onto the American public. The unfortunate aspect of this is that most people are eager to swallow these assumptions as scientific fact. Perhaps we should examine some of these.

Firstly, remember when we speak about issues involving human behavior, there is a fundamental principal that should always be kept in mind: persons are to be loved, cherished, respected, and granted their civil and human rights. That does not mean that we have to accept or approve their inappropriate behavior. If on the other hand, they have so identified themselves with their problems, and feel that you are rejecting them because of their sinful behavior, that then is their problem. We deal with this same problem with other addictive behavior such as alcoholics, gamblers, over-eaters, and shoppers. Perhaps we should include "consumers?"

Assumption number one says that homosexuality is a genetic variance of some kind that is irreversible, which leads to the conclusion that such a person has been created this way. Therefore, he or she, has the absolute right to engage in same gender sexual activity. Current research into this issue has not yet offered any proof for such an assumption. As a matter of fact some research suggests something quite different. In his fascinating book, "A Fine Young Man," Michael Gurian focuses on the biological aspects of this issue and would, therefore, favor the genetic theory.

What the studies seem to suggest is that homosexuality is not something one is born with, or conceived in, but which is acquired or learned, or imposed by one's childhood experiences. Most men and most women, who find themselves in this condition, have become so because of the deficit in their developmental process that we spoke of earlier, i.e. they have been deprived at one time, or over a long period of time, of appropriate love from the same gender parent. There are, of course, other factors that can and do contribute to or exacerbate this problem.

I refer you to two books by a British psychologist, Elizabeth Moberly, who has written on this topic. These books contain the results of her own research, study, and therapy for homosexuals, entitled "Psychogenesis and Homosexuality - A New Christian Ethic." Here she makes some very strong statements about this complex issue. One: people are not born homosexual or heterosexual. They become that way by the process of their psychic development. When the process takes place normally and naturally, the person will move into a true maturity, where he or she can relate comfortably and appropriately, with those of the opposite gender and with those of his or her own gender.

Secondly, homosexuality is not a pathology or sickness, therefore the problem. In her work, over and over, Dr. Moberly insists that homosexuality is an attempted solution to the problem, not the problem itself. The problem is the unfulfilled need that the patient or client has for same gender love. That person, yes, will remain with the problem until that need is fulfilled. It is such a powerful drive that it continuously drives the person to seek its fulfillment.

Could it be that the lack of success, in some of the therapies directed to the homosexual client, may well be due to the fact that the therapy or counseling is wasted on focusing on the attempted solution, rather than on the deep rooted deficit that creates the false solution. The theory that the condition is genetic and irreversible may be due in large part, in my opinion, to the inability of the counselor or therapist to treat such people successfully. In the face of this lack of success, it is easy to conclude that it must be a genetic problem. The psychological community must continue to study this very complex issue with real openness to the research and conclusions suggested by Dr. Moberly and others.

FEMINISM

Let us now move to a consideration of the women's movement, feminism. I am not making a direct connection here between homosexuality and feminism, but, there is a common factor, both being spinoffs, as it were, from the fatherless condition. Let me observe here that feminism has been around for a long, long time. The movement was borne out of the first stirrings of male independence following the Revolutionary War. As men, little by little, began shirking their natural responsibilities for home and society, freeing themselves from the constraints of family and church life, the women were forced to fill the gap.

In the late nineteenth century and the early twentieth century, women began to sense the urgency of the situation as more and more men were beginning to act out the independent and individualistic philosophies of the day. Women then began to band together in an attempt to correct some of the evils that were beginning to infiltrate their society. This led to the great movement for the franchise: the right to vote. Today, no one would ever suggest that women should not vote, but at that time it was taken for granted. If men had continued to function in their full role as men in society, there would have been no cause for the women to raise the voting issue.

The model that comes to mind of the feminists of that period is Carry Nation, out with her hatchet smashing in saloon windows and doors, and generally with her followers, wrecking these habitues for men. The focus of the women's movement then, unlike now, was on morality, ethics and religion. Men had abandoned their responsibilities for the moral and ethical life of the country, and now in anger and desperation they take it over. Prohibition, of course, grew out of this situation, probably not the best solution to the problem; for as it turned out, this legislation spawned a bevy of other social evils that are still with us today.

There are two observations I would make about the women's movement as it developed. I have no statistics to back this up, but it is an impression I have and I simply share it with you. You can take it or leave it.

First, the angry strident radical aspect of this movement, it would seem arises out of the absent father syndrome, the lack of masculine energy in the home over the past several generations. Women have not been named and affirmed as women by their father, and they are very angry about it. The loss of affirming love is deeply felt and there is a great unconscious and unresolved anger boiling beneath the surface. This may well account for the fact that so many celibate women are making such incredibly angry and extreme statements about church, hierarchy, about authority in general, even about God. There seems to be some kind of an obsession with patriarchy, as though it were an inherent evil invented by the devil for the express purpose of harassing women. As I will note later in this work, the real problem with patriarchy, I propose, is not in the concept, but with those who have been called to be the patriarchs, men who, like the women, have not been fathered either, and so their roles in the patriarchal system are not carried off very well. The problem here is that women are projecting this pain of their inner soul on to every male institution around, neither recognizing nor owning their own developmental deficits.

There is an uncanny perversity in the human psyche that impels one to take on the very sins we despise in the other, or perhaps we see it in ourselves and project it onto the other. This, to a great extent, occurred in the women's movement. They have long since abandoned the moralistic aims of Carry Nation and her company. In the later development of the movement, the great achievements of the now voting feminine world was the right to smoke in public, followed by the right to join the men in their bars and saloons. The exclusive men's athletic clubs became the next target for female access. At one time, the big issue was women sports writers demanding access to men's locker rooms. These are obvious inconsistencies. The tendency to emulate the sins of the alleged enemy continues. Even in the world of jobs and corporate life, women can take on the worst of masculine sinfulness. The female equipment operator on a highway construction job can swear and curse and be as vulgar as any man.

Some of the worst profanity I have ever heard, came from the mouth of a "liberated" woman. In the board rooms and offices of the big corporations, women can cheat the underdog as effectively as any man; they can exploit and impoverish whole peoples and whole nations in the interest of corporate profits. Where is the progress in all of this? Where is the equality? Where is the liberation?

When one studies the statistics, women have made tremendous strides in sharing much of public life. Women are everywhere, in every profession, in every work place. In some places, they are the majority. Yet, with all this added presence of women in the world, are we any better off? Have we improved the social and cultural health of this country in any way at all? Have we been able to gain any kind of leverage on the terrible social problems eating away at our social fabric? I think not. The problem is that women, who enter the public world, tend to leave their femininity somewhere else. Equality for them is simply being just like the man, taking on all of the man's behavioral patterns, and sins. What really is needed in the market place is not female bodies, but feminine energy.

As long as we look at the issue as one of equality, we will continue to miss the real need. To be equal in the world for the women, like any other oppressed minority, is to have what they perceived the enemy has, in this case, to be just like men, to be able to do everything a man can do. The women's movement is not about equality at all; it's about independence, individualism. This is one of the side effects of our whole educational process in this country. The feminist goal is to be as independent as men are, thus taking on another male sin.

Equality means that I have equal rights, the same rights as any one else to the opportunities to become the full person that God or nature has created me to be. It means, that as a man, I have available to me all the freedom needed to become a real man, the deep male. A woman ought to have the freedom of opportunity to become all that she is called to be as woman in this day and age. The world needs the feminine presence, the feminine energy, real female power, but not disguised in male clothes and male sins. Men need women to be truly women; and women need men to be truly men. That is the way they are created, to be in need of each other. To go our own way, whether as a man or a women is to impoverish both genders. That is the dilemma we find ourselves in today – neither gender knowing who they are, or what they should be doing.

The absence of real fatherhood, or patriarchy, is at the root of the problem, and we must be open to that assessment of the situation; look at it; study it; reflect on it; dialogue with it; clarify it; and do whatever needs to be done, to integrate that reality in our hope and plans for the human race. I certainly do not contend that women have not been oppressed, abused and mistreated. They indeed have, and that needed to be addressed and resolved. I don't think women are going about it in the right way at all, especially when they try to go it alone. The root of their problems as well as the root of men's problems is in a way twofold: the loss of true masculine energy; and the demise of authentic patriarchy in the world.

Women, and some men with them, continue to lay all their sins at the door of the Church, as patriarchy. The church really is not patriarchal in that sense. We speak of the church as Holy Mother Church, not father church. It is much more a matriarchy than a patriarchy. But because it houses the institutions of authority and discipline, under which modern men and women will inevitably complain, the deep seated anger at father finds the church a convenient target for that unresolved anger. The church is an institution, a community, a type of wagon circling for protection and security. It is the feminine principle that wants things as they were, safe and secure. It is the feminine that builds the safe nest, called home.

I think it is within the power of women, to make a significant contribution to remedy the situation we find ourselves in today. They need to stop bashing males, and begin to understand that the males hurt as much as women do. The women are called to affirm, support, and challenge the men in their lives to recover their masculine soul and become the husbands and fathers and leaders that they ought to be. We need to work together to remedy the absent father syndrome. No matter how much success that women have in equalizing themselves in the world of business, government, or even church, it won't achieve the real change needed as long as men do not know who they are.

REFLECTIONS ON BOSTON

The media had a hey-day with this issue, in spite of their obvious ignorance of the subject. With these notes, I hope I can turn our attention away from the symptomatic aspect, to the root causes. No one seems to be able to make that switch. The one item that appears here and there as a cause is the celibacy angle. That might be worth looking at, if indeed it was a problem only for single persons. Unfortunately, although not media merited, it is an issue that is across the board - other churches, other institutions, other social groupings of folks - all have their problems with this phenomenon, which we reduce to one name: pedophilia. Without going into all of the colors of this problem, I would rather address the causes, because it will apply to all the different variants of male sexuality.

The Fatherless society in which we currently live provides the environment for the development of lost males. Boys and girls alike need the father to give them gender identity. This is important, especially in their teenage years. A boy needs a strong relationship with a father; he needs to feel that he is loved by a father. When this does not occur, either because of the absent father in his home, or no other father figure has emerged in his life — he now faces life with a psychological deficit, the basis for the homosexual condition. It is quite understandable that in his search for that father's love, he would turn to male communities, e.g., the seminary or the military - with the unconscious hope that in either of these environments he will find a father to name him "man."

The Industrial Revolution. The more violent segments of the women's movement addresses themselves to the evils and dangers of patriarchy. That seemed to be the magic word in the 1970's and 1980's to call other women into the battle of the sexes. Unfortunately such warfare was quioxtic — battling windmills — since patriarchy disappeared in our culture with the Industrial Revolution — the moment, when fathers were taken from their homes early in the day and returned late in the evening - tired and stressed out. As a result, mothers began to assume much of the domestic responsibilities. I make this parenthetical observation: the women's movement was borne out of this same deficit. Many of the radicals of that time are women who are angry at their fathers — and see any kind of male authority figure as deficient and expendable.

Vatican II and the Sexual Revolution. Two great events occurred in the early 1960's that proved to be turning points in the life of the late twentieth century and which collided with each other. In the Church, there was the second Vatican Council, from which came forth sixteen critical documents for the guidance of the Church in the next millennium. In the culture, there was the moral revolution that took place centered on the West Coast in Hollywood, USC-Berkely, and Haight-Ashbury section of San Francisco. Out of this was born the religion of Secularism - which holds that only this world really counts. There is no "other world," no God, no heaven, and of course, no hell. This was a cry for unlimited freedom and that, unfortunately became for all too many the hermeneutic through which the Vatican Council documents would be interpreted, particularly the pastoral constitution "The Church in the Modern World". There was no dearth of scholars and theologians who would pursue this tack - people like Charles Curran and Hans Kung, gifted thinkers and authors, who proposed some radical and liberal ideas, that in my opinion did tremendous damage to the Church. However, it was not so much what these talented theologians suggested as answers to some of the on-going questions of the time, rather it was their followers, their disciples that took their ideas as gospel truth and church teaching. The theologian searches the Sacred Scriptures to provide deeper understanding by using idioms and language according to the times and places where he lives. He offers newer ways for understanding divine revelation. But is always the role of teaching arm of the Church, the magisterium, to teach in all matters of faith and morals. It was these over-eager followers who did the harm, both to the theologians themselves, and to the people in the church.

Consider now that most of the priests, that are in the news today for their abuse of children, were educated in seminaries that grew out of those difficult times. They were educated and formed in an environment of great confusion. There probably was not a great deal of solid spiritual direction, based on the great spiritual giants of the past; there was little or no sexual formation; and there was little, if anything at all, about the importance of healthy relationships.

Roe-Wade. In 1972, another great turning event occurs - the Supreme Court decision known as Roe-Wade - which authenticated or gave approbation to the "Pro-Choice" movement centering at that point in history, on abortion. As warned by many at the time, the effects of this have been devastating in our culture. Apart from the fact that we massacre 1.4 million babies in this country every year, which is cataclysmic in its horror — Pro Choice has become the back ground against which many social evils are developing: throwing unwanted newborns in the garbage or down the toilet; destroying handicapped and disabled children; doctor-assisted suicide; euthanasia; domestic murders; boys gunning down classmates; and why not child molesting as well. All of these ills are the consequences of this "pro choice" mentality that was spawned by the Roe-Wade decision.

Is it any wonder that the bizarre behavior was revealed by the press in the Church of Boston, and any other place where they (the media) could dig it up. From the point of view of a sociologist, all of this was probably not a big surprise. Unfortunate, sad, ugly, incredible, yes - but not unexpected.

The question that must be addressed is: "what is being done for those who are afflicted with this sickness?" I have neither seen nor read anything that would accept the responsibility for the men and women who have been victimized by the "pro-choice" philosophy of life. Our culture is obsessed with and addicted to sex. We have lost our bearings about this procreative gift of the Creator.

The solution to the issue is not easy. It will take hard work and perseverance. Our focus on the children should not deter us from the needs of the adults involved. There are rays of hope as you will see later in this work.

As the last decade of the twentieth century dawned, Robert Bly published his best selling book on manhood, entitled "Iron John." Although based on a German myth, he was able to offer some profound insights into the nature of manhood. This opened the door to a plethora of literature addressing this subject. Unfortunately, not much was done to apply these insights in a practical way for the healing of the individual male person. Book after book kept telling us what men should be, but none seem to address the "how to" part, until the men's movement of the late 1990's, entitled Promise Keepers, mentored by Bill McCartney, a coach from the University of Colorado. It was an effort to link all of this interesting sociological and psychological insights to the male spirituality.

Without knowing why or how, within our own Church, the Cursillo movement had the answer, not in the weekend itself, but in the pastoral follow up: the weekly gathering of small groups of men for prayer and sharing. Men need other men to support them in masculine issues. And this works, if the men can be honest, and trusting. This technique is at the heart of a new movement abroad today. This is a retreat program based on a book written by John Eldridge, called "Wild at Heart." This retreat program has great hope for our times, if we don't let it die. It addresses the deepest needs and issues in the masculine soul. Males will never be truly men, until they know the gifts that God and nature have given them as men. Then he can be a good man, a good husband, a good father, or a good friend.

We live in a fatherless society, and we will continue to do so with the same ramifications, until fathers are really fathers, and they cannot be fathers until they are really men. Manhood, as given to us by our creator has been mishandled and mistreated by the culture all too long. The health of our nation, the health of our families, and the health of the Church is at stake here.

PEDOPHILIA

Here we have another phenomenon not generally understood, where we tend to rely on the secular press for understanding. It would appear that the press has relied entirely on Webster's definition of this term: "a sexual perversion in which children are the preferred sexual object." That, it seems to me, is a very narrow understanding of that term, because it is synonymous with the term, child molestation. Not so, like homosexuality itself, this too is a coat of several colors. Pedophilia is a Greek-rooted term from *pais* meaning child and *philia* meaning love, or friendship. Thus we have love of, or friendship with a child. That, it would appear, opens us up to a variety of ways in which that love or friendship is manifested. A man or woman who simply loves teaching young children would, by definition, be a pedophile. A man who loves coaching Little League baseball would also be a pedophile. A gifted woman musician, who enjoys forming and directing children's choirs or orchestras, is a pedophile in that sense.

Even a grandfather who has a great relationship with his grandchildren, who enjoy his company, like to sit on his lap, and receive tasty snacks from him, would be a pedophile. Between the folks mentioned here and the ones the media consistently portrays is a long gap possibly filled with a number of levels in this love-friendship attraction to children. My point in bringing this up is once again a warning, a caution, on how we use the language.

In the Roman Catholic tradition, the newly ordained priest is committed to a life time of celibacy, i.e., the foregoing of a family of his own. Arriving at this point of his life, perhaps still in his mid-twenties, he enters upon his mission with a high level of testosterone, sexual

57

energy. This doesn't mean he has created for himself the agony of restraint from all sexual activity. Out of that same reservoir of high energy, he can immerse himself in all the different aspects of clerical ministry. Among these there is often the case that he is charged with the oversight of a number of youth activities – religious instruction, athletic teams, boys' choir or altar servers, Boy Scouts. In these activities he comes into contact with a lot of young boys and girls.

This same energy generates the desire for progeny, to be a father. The fulfillment of this desire finds itself in his relationship to the boys in these various programs. His formation and training in the seminary should have prepared him for this work, which does have some dangers. He should know how one forms healthy relationships with women, with his peers, and with the children to which he is called to minister.

Occasionally, he will encounter someone, perhaps a youngster who has deep needs. In his effort to resolve these needs, he may become emotionally involved with this boy. Lacking fathering in his own family, the boy begins to cling to this "father." We now have a situation of two people, each of which has an honest need: the priest to be a father; the youngster to have a father. Without well established boundaries in the relationship, it can disintegrate into erotic and even genital behavior. Now each one has a terrible problem: the priest with his violation of the chastity with which he has promised to live out his celibate commitment; and the child who does not have a place or person to approach with his concern about this relationship.

If we look back in the family history of these priests and that of the victims, we will discover a lot of dysfunction. The priest's own father did not lead his son to manhood, or may even have sexually abused him. What this suggests is that we may not have screened seminary candidates, not to eliminate them, but to heal them. The priest-to-be should have been trained to assess such problems in the children under his care, and help them to enter into a healing process.

THE GREATEST GENERATION

This may seem a bit out of order here, but there is an aspect of this sociological phenomenon, which ten years ago, Tom Brokaw, under that title, produced a memoir of folks who lived through the great depression, the second world war with all of its challenges, and the period of reconstruction that followed. Since I was part of that generation I relished his portrayal of the men and women who banded together to support President Roosevelt and his "New Deal," overcoming some of the worst phases of the depression.

In 1939 Europe was embroiled in the conflict that was instigated by Adolph Hitler and his Third Reich. By partnering with Mussolini in Italy and the leadership in Japan, Hitler planned to take over the whole world. Late in 1941 Japan bombed our fleet stationed at Pearl Harbor in the Hawaiian Islands, which brought us into this international conflict.

The entire country was then mobilized to meet this threat. Hundreds of thousands of young men abandoned schools, jobs, or careers to enlist in one of the armed forces, creating the largest military in our history. For four years the nation's focus was on the war effort.

The conflict in Europe ended in the Spring of 1944, but the struggle continued in the Pacific. Finally in mid-August of 1945, after Hiroshima and Nagasaki had been destroyed by A-bombs, the war came to an end. The use of this new weapon of destruction was not our finest hour, but what followed the peace treaty was a redemption of that awful event.

Both Germany and Japan became beneficiaries of the Marshall Plan, an organized effort on the part of the allies to help with the reconstruction of the axis nations, bringing them back into the family of nations, restoring their economic base, and repairing much of the devastation of wartime.

All of these events came to happy conclusions because of the generous application of manly wisdom and power.

Today, our nation stands in the shadow of events like 9/11 and Katrina and are practically paralyzed in our efforts to respond. Katrina is nothing compared with the vast destruction of World War II, and yet we can't seem to get our act together and rescue the people and property devastated by that very unusual hurricane. Why? There are no real men around to join together, roll up their sleeves, and get to work. No, we are too busy in the blame games and the "Let George do it" game. Nor can we discount the race factor here either. We do not have enough manhood, because we do not have enough real fathers, carrying out their normal responsibilities vis-a-vis their sons and daughters.

Looking back now through that half of a century of history, we can see that the "Greatest Generation," had a dark side to it. Many of the men who formed this famous generation, keenly aware of the struggles they endured during those years vowed, perhaps unconsciously, that his children would not have to experience these same inconveniences: hunger, poverty, unemployment, soup lines, war, rationing, etc. They didn't seem to be aware of the reality that it was these very things that ripened them into manhood, and subsequently gave them the energy, the courage, the perseverance to accomplish that which not only brought an end to each of these challenges, but also helped to enrich the culture of America.

Many of these young men, returning home to an uncertain future were aided by their government to acquire a college education through the GI Bill of Rights,that provided grants to returning veterans. In this way these men were able to enter into professions and careers that would provide the resources to raise and educate a family. In their effort to protect their offspring from the evils they had endured, they weren't necessarily doing their children a favor.

This next generation were not handed down the solid values that made their fathers "great." Instead they were handed down all the latest toys and games. Yes, all went to college and were able to acquire the knowledge and skills to find good employment, which often positioned them to enter the world of corporate capitalism and be awarded unbelievable compensatory salaries and perks. In the meantime they have by-passed all those moments or events that would have helped them to enter into healthy manhood. Too many of them have chosen to remain in the adolescent state. Not that they wanted to do that, but there weren't the fathers, or other men around as role models, to show them the way out of adolescence into a healthy and productive manhood. They continue to play their adolescent games, which the public witnesses every night on the news. No better evidence of this exists today than what we are presently involved in as we search for a new president of our country. Not only the campaign games we've been watching for all too long, but even the business of congress itself, all too often, descends into adolescent game playing.

Yes, this is the dark side of a great gift that the Greatest Generation was for our country. Our task is to allow the methods and means of rediscovering our manhood and our womanhood to once again emerge in our culture. Maybe then we will be able to get the job done, whether it be the people's business in congress, or the devastation of Katrina, or the terrorism that appears to threaten us. But I think we need to add this to the challenge of HIV/AIDS and GLOBAL WARMING.

This collection of these issues among others stand out in their relationship to a vanishing manhood and the accompanying reality of the absent father. We will now move into some anthropological reflections that will put us in touch with the deep-seated roots of the problem.

HUMAN ORIGINS

At this point we will focus our attention on the origins of the human race, the human family, both through the eyes of science and Sacred Scripture. I do not intend to become involved in the current controversy regarding the origins of life on our planet: Creationism, Evolution, or Intelligent Design. We do need to look at the deepest meanings of what it was to be a human being, to be a man, to be a woman. What were the fundamental qualities or attributes that characterized each gender as we emerged from the original creative act? What are the things that characterize maleness or femaleness? Are there constitutive elements that are distinctive for each gender?

THE CULTURAL VIEW OF HOMO SAPIENS

We begin by examining the most elementary myths and archaeological findings that relate to the origins of the human species, and see what they tell us about the nature of man and of woman.

Traveling in the ancient world, particularly in the middle east where the origins of the human species occurred, one may have the opportunity to visit some of the museums and archaeological sites available there. You will be exposed to ancient artifacts that represent the human genitalia. Large stone representations of the erect male organ are found in the cultures that go back as far as 15,000 B.C. and as recent as the first century before our era. My first encounter with these ancient artifacts

63

was somewhat discomforting and I quickly made some negative moral judgments about that long ago culture. As I continued to read and study these origins, I came to understand what was really going on with these people. For primitive peoples, there seemed to be an awareness that new life was achieved by the union of male and female in the sexual encounter. For them this was mystery – a profound mystery, something of divine significance. Whoever this supreme power or force in the world was, must be the power of life itself. They were also ready to recognize that their lives were in the hands of powers beyond themselves. This power, whoever or whatever it was, was like a giant phallus. To them these carved images were a reminder of a creative power coming from on high. Along with penile representations, some of these ancient folks carved circles, donut shaped, to represent the womb. They may have been designed together in union or separately.

In contrast to these simple people, whose wisdom far surpasses our own, we, in the western world have made gods of our genitals. By our obsessive behavior we tend to worship our genitals as it were. They seem to have become the source of supreme good for us, namely, pleasure, or self-gratification. It is very difficult, for men and women of current Western culture, to reflect on their bodies in terms of primitive and universal truths about themselves. We are so caught up in the compulsion of pleasure, we can see nothing else. Primitive man perceived or intuited sexuality in ultimate terms. For them, it was a god-image; modern man, especially an American, separates genitality from sexuality. There is no ultimacy to it. We are concerned only for the immediate pleasure that it offers.[4]

---

4   cf. "Phallos, the Sacred Image of the Masculine" by Eugene Monich; also "The Phallic Quest" by James Wyly

For us to understand the difference between male and female, between masculine and feminine, we need to probe into these primitive meanings of sexuality. What is a human, and what are the very basic energies that form human beings and give purpose and direction to life? What are the things that distinguish maleness and femaleness? Which, among these are interchangeable, and which are not?

It is very difficult to treat the topic of fatherlessness without a whole session on human sexuality, because the two issues are so intimately related. But that is not our scope here to do that. Let me, however, make two important observations about human sexuality: first, modern society has completely lost the fundamental understanding of what sex is really all about. Sexuality is a life urge, its primary focus being reproduction, the continuation of the human species. It is a survival urge, i.e., the survival of human kind on the planet. What our hedonistic culture has done, is turn it all upside down, and make pleasure or self-gratification as the central focus of sex and the reproductive aspect, an undesirable accident. The drive or urge, even the fascination within the human person for sexual activity is not primarily for pleasure, but for species survival. In that, we are not unlike other mammals. The pleasure is an important part of the experience, of course, which in its way helps to guarantee the survival aspect.

The second thing to be aware of is that the modern culture has perverted the whole process by focusing exclusively on the genitals, making it the totality of human sexuality. This is one great example of reductionism – reducing the whole to one of its parts. In a sense it is a mistake to speak of male sex or female sex. There is only one sex: human sex, which fulfills its basic function when the two components come together. That need not be in a genital experience at all. Unity among the genders (and

I prefer to use the word gender, rather than sex, for the reason stated above) is achieved on many levels other than the physical or biological.

Let us then symbolize sexuality in this way. First, draw a straight line across a board and make it an arrow, which represents the male or masculine; now draw a circle which will represent the female or feminine. This straight arrow symbolizes the male phallus (the erect penis); which the arrow in the circle represents the womb. Masculine power at this fundamental level is called "phallic"; the feminine power is called "wombic." These terms, used by anthropologists, describe those special powers that are peculiar to humanity as males or females. As important as the genitals are for species survival, they also have a symbolic importance for other aspects of the human personality, namely, the psychic and spiritual qualities of our sexuality that lie deep within us. Let us explore some of these.

In a stereotypical western movie, there will be a wagon train on its way to Oregon Territory, crossing the great plains. Over and over, they encounter some of the native peoples that inhabit this land. Some are friendly and allow the passage, but others are quite hostile and present some challenging encounters. Having arrived at the foothills of the Rocky Mountains, the scouts discover there are Indian scouts keeping track of them on a distant bluff. What can these frontiersmen now do? They could immediately go out and do in the scouts, confront the enemy and overpower him, or they could dialogue and negotiate safe passage through their lands. On the other hand, they could circle the wagons (creating a safe womb) to protect themselves against this possible enemy attack. Addressing the problem head on and dialoguing with it, is the masculine approach; circling the wagons and securing the folks inside is the feminine approach. It isn't that one approach is right and the other wrong. The individual situation, and circumstances surrounding the event will dictate how best to approach it, which must be the focus of our discernment in the matter. Here, as in many other matters, we realize that our decisions do not always have black and white answers.

Now we move to a very important element in our discussion. When does one experience the fullness of male energy or female energy? It would appear that this occurs at the time of the genital encounter, at the point of creating new life, fulfilling, as it were, the fundamental purpose of human sexuality. The male is fully male when in erection; the female most fully female when in ovulation. Look deeply at this very important event in the sexual relationship, and one can see that the qualities of the physical organs at that moment, symbolize at the same time the qualities or characteristics that lie deep within the psyche and spirit of the human person.

In this treatment, we are particularly interested in the qualities of manhood, and so we will center our focus on the masculine qualities. Yet, they cannot be fully understood without some perception of the feminine qualities which we will briefly include. Here we look for those characteristics of male sexual arousal, the phallus. The first thing men are aware of is that it is spontaneous. It comes and goes almost on its own will. It can occur, of course, through physical manipulation, or erotic fantasies, but it can occur without any help from the person himself, as it regularly does during sleep times. This frequent spontaneity leads us to observe that one of the male characteristics is spontaneity.

Secondly, the most obvious thing about the phallus is that it is firm or hard, created by the blood that has invaded the flaccid penis which is necessary for the complete encounter with the female. From this we observe those qualities, suggested by this, for other levels of human living: instead of hard, we would offer aggressive, courageous, strong, and power. This then moves us to the third aspect - penetration. This symbolizes the qualities of directness, frankness, incisiveness or in common parlance, "no beating around the bush!"

The next aspect is the discharge of the seminal fluid that carries the seed of life into the womb to find its way to the ovum. This is the moment of creativity, another male quality we can look at. On this physical or biological level, it means new birth of another of the species, but on the psychological and spiritual level, there are other ways in which we see new life created, and man will be at the heart of this as well, which we will see later on.

Finally, and this is just as important as all the others in terms of defining masculinity. Once the creative act is complete, the phallus wanes or recedes, and the phallus becomes flaccid again. This is a sign of death or completion, or of simply letting go. What it says about a male is that he must be willing to die to a lot of things, and move on to others. He must let go, and let die, that which he treasures now, so as to move on to something more or even better.

In contradistinction to these qualities, the female exhibits those peculiar to her. Without going into them in the same detail as with the male, let us briefly describe them: Ovulation is normally predictable and cannot be induced, prompting us to observe that regularity is the feminine quality that complements the spontaneity of the male; Softness or gentleness, the quality that complements the hardness quality of the male; Complementing the penetration of the male, there is the "receptivity" of the woman. The semen he creates and discharges is now received and nurtured by the female. Finally, in the female we see "connectedness" and "continuity" complementing the male "finality."

These are some, among many, of the qualities for each of these energies, both of which are truly human energies, but complementary. I would further suggest that these qualities are essential to each gender and if they are frustrated or short-circuited in any way, manhood and womanhood suffer diminishment or sickness. The male must be allowed to manifest these qualities to be at home with his maleness, and the female must be allowed to manifest her qualities in order to be at home with her femaleness.

With these observations before us, we might conclude that a sense of purpose or fulfillment doesn't have to be on the procreative level at all. Fulfillment can be experienced just as adequately on the social, psychic, or spiritual levels as well. But now let us move on to the Biblical Anthropology.

REFLECTION V

BIBLICAL ANTHROPOLOGY

Sometime after the origins of the human race were well established, it would seem that the male became so fascinated with his maleness, especially his phallic energies, that it over-inflated his ego. This led him to view all of reality through a phallic prism, prompting him to name that reality in masculine terms, ignoring the fact or truth that the wombic and feminine were equally important.

What God seems to be doing in the revelation we are about to look at in the Book of Genesis is a corrective – a revelation to bring back the balance between the male and the female, to bring them together again and demonstrating that they really belong together. How effective that was in the beginning or how long it actually lasted, the Genesis story does not reveal to us. Somehow, it would seem, that man could not really hear what was being said, the inflation was too deeply imbedded in the psyche.

In the women's movement we have this cry from the depths of their being for that unity, that equality, and that togetherness they sense should be there. We do not often find that in their rhetoric, which tends to be pretty superficial. Underneath their anger is that eternal longing to be one with the male, to truly image the God who made them.

In the Biblical story of creation, which we read in the Book of Genesis, we have two accounts of the creation of man (i.e., human being). One account is in the first chapter, the other in the second chapter and they are remarkably different. The original author of Genesis, perhaps, had gathered together cultural myths of the middle east that best expressed for his readers or listeners how they perceived the origins of the universe, and also the origins of human life. These are important texts for us as we pursue our search for the meaning of who we are.

First, Genesis 1:26-31

Then God said, 'let us make man in our own image, after our own likeness. Let them have dominion over the fish of the sea, the birds of the air, and the cattle, and over all the wild animals and all the creatures that crawl on the ground.' God created man in his image; in the divine image he created him; male and female he created them. God blessed them, saying 'Be fertile and multiply; fill the earth and subdue it'. .and so it happened. God looked at everything he had made and found it very good.

Second, Genesis 2:7-9, 15-25

The Lord God formed man out of the clay of the ground and blew into his nostrils the breath of life, and so man became a living being. Then the Lord God planted a garden in Eden, in the east, and he placed there the man whom he had formed. Out of the ground the Lord God made various trees to grow that were delightful to look at and good for food, with the tree of life in the middle of the garden and the tree of knowledge of good and bad. . . The Lord God then took the man and settled him in the garden of Eden, to cultivate and care for it. The Lord God gave man this order: 'you are free to eat from any of the trees of the garden except the tree of knowledge of good and bad. From that tree you shall not eat; the moment you eat from it you are surely doomed to die.'

The Lord said 'it is not good for man to be alone. I will make a suitable partner for him.' So the Lord God formed out of the ground various wild animals and various birds of the air, and he brought them to the man to see what he would call them; whatever the man called each of them would be its name. The man gave names to all the cattle, all the birds of the air, and all the wild animals; but none proved to be the suitable partner for man.

So the Lord God cast a deep sleep on the man, and while he was asleep, he took out one of his ribs and closed up its place with flesh. The Lord God then built up into a woman the rib that he had taken from the man. When he brought her to the man, the man said: 'This one, at last, is bone of my bones and flesh of my flesh; this one shall be called woman for out of her man this one has been taken.' That is why a man leaves his father and mother and clings to his wife, and the two of them become one body. The man and his wife were both naked, yet they felt no shame.[5]

As we grew up, most of us came to understand these passages about God strictly in masculine terms, and so he is; but when we examine the passages from Genesis more carefully, we discover that God must also be feminine, and so she is. The image of God in which human being was created includes both, it would seem: "let us create man in our image, male and female he created them." The image of God is filled with both traditional masculine attributes as well as the traditional feminine ones. When we read the Psalms with an openness to this understanding, we will discover all kinds of qualities that were used to describe God in the Old Testament, as not particularly male in our traditional understanding of maleness. Compassion, tenderness, gentleness, mercy and affection are seen there as descriptive of Jahweh-God. God the Father is the author of life, but isn't that a combined role, initiating life and bringing it forth? He is seen as providing for and sustaining this life, another joint activity or role.

5   All Scripture references are taken from "New American Bible," Giant Print Ed., World Catholic Press.

As a consequence of this broader understanding, of the creator that we are talking about here, can we not perceive a Father who includes within his being, all that is both masculine and feminine – motherly as well as fatherly? God is, from this understanding, an androgynous being (coming from two Greek words: *ANDROS and GYNE* – man and woman). This God of ours incorporates in his existence, all that is best of the masculine and all that is best of the feminine. Most of our personal experience of human fatherhood has been pretty much a distorted masculine one, and similarly much of our experience of motherhood is likewise very disfigured. As we can see, we must revise our understanding of God before we can relate to him in any authentic biblical or Christian way.

When we think of ourselves as being made in the image and likeness of God, it is not in our separateness or individuality that we image the Creator, but in our togetherness. It is in the bonded complementarity of maleness and femaleness that we most accurately reflect the image of God. What we have to do, as we dig deeper into this biblical understanding, is prepare ourselves to accept a more authentic awareness of God's fatherhood in our lives. We need to take all that is the best in our father image and all that is best in our mother image and ascribe it to God. In this way we will begin to have some kind of a clue as to who this Father/Mother God truly is – the God who calls us to union with, and in him/her.

The most accurate thing we can say at this point is that God transcends our categories, especially these gender distinctions. We humans use such terms analogically to help us understand God as best we can. We need a new language to talk about God, but it will still have to be personal. The problem I have with inclusive language, that is being suggested in order to de-sex the scriptures, is that it depersonalizes God with the consequence of making God less real and less approachable.

What we come to see in terms of relationship between man and woman is that they are partners in the on-going creative power of God. For it is written "be fertile and multiply; fill the earth and subdue it." (Gen. 1:28) In the perfection of their original existence, as they came forth from the hand of God, they were equal partners in this creative enterprise. It is only after the Fall that we have a description of the division of roles. (Cf. Gen. 3:16-29) Much of what we complain about today in the relationship of roles is a result of sin, not of creation. What human progress, spirituality, and Christian growth is called to do is to help us move to retrieve that which was lost through original and personal sin. The whole of God's salvific plan focuses on reuniting all that was divided in the Eden tragedy. God sends forth his own spirit to work in the human heart, and in social groupings of men and women in the Church and in the world around us, to bring about that unity that was promised. If we are not plugged into the Spirit of God, if we are not graced by the divine presence, we are bound to multiply our own disunity. We need to face the fact that what is going on in our culture today, even in religious circles, is in truth creating even more disunity. The world today is in deterioration, because it has lost contact with the Father, the true source of our masculine energy and power.

With all of this as a background, let us move now to examine how this has affected the history of the human race, the people of God, and contemporary life. In the beginning, God (or nature, if you wish) was seen as the creative energy that gave to all being, existence and its meaning. The earth and the universe were the vast feminine womb that received that new life. In Jesus, we see a new insertion of God into the world – bringing again new life. The church is the womb in which that life is nurtured. We can see this dramatically expressed in symbol in the Easter

Vigil service, when the giant candle is plunged into the large container of water. This is a powerful sexual symbol, the giant phallus that is God being plunged into the womb of humanity.

As we examine the qualities represented by the phallus and the womb, one thing that we should be conscious of now is that the basic thrust of phallic life is TO GIVE; on the other side, the basic wombic thrust is TO RECEIVE. We are compelled to conclude that the primal masculine energy is that of GIVING, while the primal feminine energy is RECEIVING. When mankind fell away from the primeval innocence, they headed down a path that led only to themselves. We see this expressed in the temptation of the serpent as he says to Eve, ". . .you will be like gods." Our culture today has capitalized on that self-seeking urge, encourages it, and affirms it. When self becomes God, the primal energies are mutated, as it were, into TAKING energy. So that instead of GIVING and RECEIVING energies that complement each other, we now have both male and female absorbed in TAKING energy, ending up in competition with each other.

Everyone's attitude toward life today is one "what can I get out of it?" In other words, "what can I take for myself?" If you can't see that or even take my word for it, look at the language we use every day. Note the many idioms that are commonly used in everyday parlance that tend to support this whole idea of taking, creating as it does, a very individualistic and self-approach to all of reality. Here are some of these idioms: "take your time; take a walk; take a bath, etc." There are hundreds of these idioms we use every day. When we stop to analyze these expressions, they really have little meaning; in fact some are ludicrous. Why couldn't it be just as easily said "give myself to walking, to bathing, to drinking," or whatever? But no, we have to take it. We don't give, we don't receive. We just take.

In a taking culture the fundamental phallic and wombic energies are unable to operate in a healthy way. That is why we have this vast reservoir of resentment and anger building up in the unconscious life of the human race. Men and women remain unfulfilled because they cannot be who they are, they cannot be their true selves. Everyone is taking! No giving, no receiving.

In the great advances of civilization and religion, what happened was a great outpouring or explosion of phallic power, a great giving off of masculine energy that created something new, and this poured out new seeds of life on the planet, from men like Plato and Aristotle; Augustine and Aquinas; Columbus and Magellan; Copernicus and Galileo; Roentgen and Curie; Lister and Pasteur. These and many others, even into our own time and in all areas of human endeavor, have enriched the lives of all of us by their contribution, and what have we done? We have TAKEN those, not received them, for our own selfish purposes. Too often the great break-throughs of science and technology today are being used, not to sow seeds of life, but to kill, to maim, and to destroy.

These great people of the past were men, and in some cases even women, exhibiting great GIVING energy. The function of the RECEIVING energy is to receive that seed, nurture it, support it, protect it, so that it has continuity and connectedness with the rest of life. Our problem today is that we do not see such energy as creative or positive. Whenever a change emerges on the horizon it is usually viewed as the enemy.

Often the seeds of new life are destroyed or not received at all; other times the seeds themselves overcome the obstacles and take root. We see this in the Civil Rights movement of the 1960's and 1970's. A man like Martin Luther King, Jr., who emerged on the American scene with tremendous phallic energy, and sowed the seeds of new life for racially discriminated people. And what did the white community do with that? What was their response? Circle the wagons, call out the police, bring in the dogs, to protect the status quo. Some of those seeds, however, were not despoiled by such blindness and bigotry, but took root and continued to produce fruit and a new generation of seed sowers.

The sad reality here is that some, even among those who were objects of persecution, tended to take this new life and encircle it with all kinds of safe fencing, rather than allowing it to go with the wind and be seeded in other places. That is what we call institutionalization.

Let me give you another example from the Church. In 1958, Pope John XXIII exhibited a profound display of phallic energy in calling the second Vatican Council. This was certainly an energy that was very spontaneous, deeply penetrating, creative and life-giving, to be sure. What was the response of the church? Circle the wagons! Later the entire pontificate of Paul VI was an ongoing struggle to keep the wagons on the trail and headed in the direction the Spirit had marked out in the Council. John Paul II continued this effort. But even in the midst of his long and fruitful reign, there was more wagon circling going on which continues to this very day.

Our problem is not whether there should be one kind of energy or the other. Our task lies in creating the right balance, to have each functioning in its proper time and place. We have to be receptive to new life; that new life needs nurturance. Therefore, it needs a womb, a place in which it is nurtured, and that means institutional or community life. Here the seeds are received, the new ideas, the new methods, and the new principles. Here they are nurtured and purified and brought to birth. At the same time the institution or community must be open to the phallic or 'giving' energy, which will guide it and renew it, and this means an openness to prophets and reformers.

Today, the situation is so very critical because we have depleted our store of masculine energy or phallic power. The home, the family, the society itself is being destroyed. All of the supportive elements of our culture are disintegrating: our schools, government, law and order, medicine, and yes, church. No aspect of societal life has been spared. We are on the point of completely destroying ourselves. As has been said before, it won't take a nuclear war to destroy the human race, we are already well on the way to an annihilation of a different kind. Here in America, for example, we have a population growth rate geared to extinction. If it were not for the influx of immigrants from Latin America and the Orient, our population would have been significantly lower in the last census than at any time since World War II. You might be aware that we've done a lot of wagon circling in regards to immigration, as we note in much of the rhetoric surrounding this issue today.

This now leads us to some concluding observations and suggestions. In the process we have described, we arrive at a point where the power of the masculine soul has been emasculated; could it be on the way to some kind of psychic death? When men have lost their creativity, their spontaneity, their sense of worth, and if they cannot be true fathers to their sons and their daughters, these offspring become confused and terribly frustrated. There is a caution here: it happens deep within us, and we rarely have any conscious realization that it is going on.

The last level of maleness is now being wiped out by the cultural switch to "recreational sex" in which contraception, sterilization, and abortion play a significant role. It is unfortunate, but the hedonistic philosophy, by which most of our countrymen live, forms the values and attitudes of the culture. This is at the root of much of the violence we see in the world today. It is the fruit of the perversity of sin itself. When the man cannot function according to his phallic urges, he creates new symbols to express his manhood. This is not something especially new, nor is our situation all that new either. We just happen to be more aware of it because of our advanced informational technology, and it is a universal phenomenon. As we all know we have at our finger tips the power to destroy ourselves and the whole planet with us, simply by flipping a switch. That makes the situation much more frightening. The interesting aspect of the situation is that the new symbols man makes for himself are not particularly creative or life giving. They tend to be destructive and death-dealing instead. This tends to parallel the cultural switch from that of life to death – "the culture of death."

There are a number of phallic symbols for the American male today, but let me share something about one of them which, for a majority of the male population, is an important male symbol. I speak of the rifle. Look at the rifle. It is everything a man wants: hardness, penetrability, seed sowing (pellets of lead that deal only death). There is nothing life-giving about a rifle, save the fact that it can be a means to provide food for the family. There is one quality lacking. It does not shrivel up and become flaccid, instead it is ready to go again and again. The larger the gun and the more automatic it is, the more manly energy the man feels.

One of the most, if not the most, difficult obstacle in our efforts to curtail crime in this country is the "lobby" that works for the National Rifle Association. Every attempt, by anyone or institution to regulate, limit, or control fire arms in any way whatever is immediately attacked by this lobby. Why? Are they so concerned about life and property with their appeal to the "Bill of Rights" which they too often misrepresent? What they really are protecting is their maleness, the gun that is a sign of manhood. It is a power symbol of control. Legislation directed toward limiting or controlling this symbol is viewed not as an attack on freedom so much as an attack on their maleness, not necessarily their manhood. Again one needs to understand that this all goes on in the deep unconscious. Most men are not aware that they are doing this.

This is all part of the denial syndrome referred to earlier. Males need to bring forth from their unconscious these issues, and deal with them, understand them, and allow them to be healed. Hiding them in the shadow side of the personality only prevents the male person from moving out of his adolescence into true manhood. Of course there are many examples of men who have managed this aspect of their lives, and are now functioning as mature men, husbands and fathers. They provide the examples or models for others.

MAKING CONNECTIONS
[Bringing It All Together]

Having reflected on man as a sexual being, let us now see how it connects with his spirituality. Only when the human person can view himself in the totality of his being, embracing all that he is, including his own dark side and sinful inclinations, he will always wobble around on a lame spirituality of some kind. Males have a basic spirituality that is in harmony with their nature as males, their deepest qualities. Masculine spirituality is characterized by the phallic qualities that we outlined earlier. Because of the influence our history and culture have had on the man, he seems incapable of living out his natural spirituality.

What I maintain in this chapter is that our spirituality (and this would be true for the woman as well) is very much influenced by and woven together with our sexuality. We already have seen how our sexual nature defines how we react to, and respond to, reality. The problem here, however, is that for many, many centuries we have been influenced by the Augustinian psychology, which described man as a being made up of body and soul, the material and the spiritual. These aspects of his being were seen as distinct from one another. For centuries, Christians were far more interested in "saving souls" than in ministering to bodies. Sexuality was a function of the body, while spirituality was a function of the soul. Christian psychology today has moved away from this Augustinian paradigm, clearing the way for a more holistic view of our manhood, our true human nature. This holistic view of man recognizes the interdependency and interaction between all of the aspects of the personality.

Another obstacle to our wholesome understanding of the relationship between sexuality and spirituality is the present hedonism that influences so much of our behavior, most especially our sexuality. In order to have a healthy attitude toward sex, this gift must be seen in its most primitive dimension, namely as a life force, a life impulse, the preservation of the species. When that view of sexuality is exchanged for one that sees it only as a pleasure impulse, we will find ourselves back into the old Augustinian model, the separation of sexuality from spirituality.

In order to understand the real nature of our own spirituality, we need to look at the human personality in its totality. There are many ways we can describe the personality; many diagrams that we can use to help understand how the various aspects of the human person are connected with one another. Somewhere I came across this diagram illustrating different aspects of the personality. We begin with a circle, which we divide into three equal segments representing: a)gut; b)heart; c)head. The gut represents the earliest relationship we have with reality – our basic instincts, the spontaneous response we have to any stimulus we encounter. The heart represents the subjective aspects of who we are, our emotions and passions. This is the second level of response to reality. And thirdly, the head, representing the rational and volitional aspects of our interplay with reality. Most folks in the field tend to stop here and limit personality to these three elements. I feel that it is important to recognize that the BODY is also a part of the personality and as such be included here, represented by the circle itself. The person that we are is housed in a body created by nature or God. For Christian psychologists and Jungians, there is a fourth dimension or element of the human personality, which we call the spirit. It is the human spirit that appears at the center of our diagram, holding, as it were, the other three elements together, like the hub that holds together the spokes of the wheel.

Spirituality plays that role for us. It is the binding force that struggles to keep the rest of our personality in balance. If we were to go more deeply into this, and look at the various ways in which different schools type personalities, the one thing we would discover is that our personality will be pretty much determined by the emphasis we place on one of the basic elements. We tend to live out of one of the aspects more than the others. For example, the person who lives out of his head is very rational about everything. For him reality is only what he can account for in his head, or reason. The heart person, on the other hand tends to live out of his feelings and emotions and relates to reality in a very subjective way, by how he feels about it. The instinctual person responds to reality from his gut, without reasoning or feeling. He simply responds spontaneously. The human spirit's role is not to establish an area of its own, but to be the binding force for all the others, and to keep them in some kind of balance. As this occurs, we develop a more balanced approach to reality.

What do we mean by spirituality? Spirituality is the recognition and acceptance of certain assumptions by which we answer the basic questions of our existence: who am I? where did I come from? where am I going? and how do I get there? Christian spirituality is based on the assumptions that Jesus Christ is true God and true man, that he took on our flesh, he left us a message, he died a violent death, was resurrected on the third day, ascended into heaven, and sent his Holy Spirit to be with his followers. You may recognize these as the articles of our Christian Creed, the very fundamental truths of Christianity.

Christian masculine spirituality will rest on these assumptions, to be sure, but how that spirituality expresses and celebrates the assumptions will be unique to each man.

We shall now see how the same qualities that were derived from an examination of the physical act of reproduction, will apply here also: First, spontaneity. When a man is freed up from the constrictions of institutional life, he is very open to and naturally enjoys a spontaneous approach to God. We see this in the Cursillo movement and in the Charismatic experience in its early flowering. "It is so much fun to be a Christian when you can be yourself, your true self," a quote often heard at that time.

Secondly, it must be an aggressive spirituality, one that attacks, that confronts, that gives. I think that male spirituality, above all else, is a giving spirituality. If we look at the lives of the great saints of our tradition, the thing that stands out is their willingness to surrender everything to God, to the Church, to the spread of the Gospel. In this light, I think of St. Paul who certainly gave his all to preach "Jesus Christ and Him Crucified;" I think of the other apostles, all of whom gave their very lives in the cause and work of proclaiming the Good News of Jesus Christ to the world. I think of the Fathers of the Church, those early writers who created the solid foundations of church literature, interpreting the Jesus event and the Gospel, which has been the source of Christian understanding of our faith ever since. I think of the great philosophers and theologians, such as Augustine and Aquinas, who produced prodigious reflections on those very questions of ultimacy that spirituality ought to address. I think of the great founders of Religious Orders, who saw a need and catalyzed a group of followers to meet those needs – men like Benedict, Francis, Dominic, Bernard of Clairvaux, and Vincent de Paul. I think of the great Bishops, who gave themselves unstintingly in the pastoral charge that they accepted and diligently carried out. I think also of the great missionaries in every age, who went to the corners of the earth to announce the good news. Masculine spirituality is truly a giving spirituality, aggressive and creative.

Thirdly, the spirituality of the male must be a penetrating spirituality, one that inserts itself into both the life of the church and the life of the world. It is clear and direct, not at all like most of the spirituality we are exposed to today. For example, there were two foci to the Cursillo movement: one, to develop leadership among lay men in the church, and two, to Christianize environments. Both of these are masculine energies.

Fourthly, it is spirituality that gives life, that creates something new in the church and for the world; there is something about masculine spirituality that invigorates others, bringing them to a new way of life themselves. Male witness and testimony is often more inspiring and motivating than the feminine. Perhaps this is true because we aren't exposed to it all that often.

Fifthly and finally, masculine spirituality is open to death: death itself, death to my opinions; death to this neat thing I am doing today; death to this prayer movement; and death to this apostolate. Masculine spirituality enables the male to "let go and let God." The male is open to God's call to move on to another place, to another work, to another ministry. Here, we might think of the great patriarchs and prophets of the Old Testament: Abraham, Moses, David, Jonah, and Jeremiah. In the Christian era, there was Paul of Tarsus, Irenaeus, Francis, and Ignatius. In our own time we might mention John Paul II, Oscar Romero, even Martin Luther King, Jr.

Recall for a moment our frontier allegory, the scene where circling the wagons for protection was an expression of a feminine response. The church, as we have known it for a long, long time is very much in the circular mode, the nesting mode, the security mode, whatever you want to call it, but it is definitely a feminine context. That is not sufficient if that is all church can mean. The problems with the church is that the males who run it may not be deeply masculine. They are products of the feminization process as much as any other male in society today. They have not been given their true masculine soul. Thus, their exercise of ministry in the church will be along feminine lines, i.e., the safe and secure lines. There is no room in such a church for adventure or risk taking.

However, let me point out here that the Popes of the twentieth century did not fit this model. Beginning with Pius XII we have experienced leadership at the very top that was not reluctant to be aggressive, creative, even adventuresome. Pius XII laid the ground work for the Vatican Council with three challenging encyclicals: "Divino Afflante Spiritu" in which he opened up scripture study to scholars; encouraged the reading and reflection on the Word of God by all people in the church; "Mediator Dei" in which he laid the principles for the liturgical renewal of Vatican II; and "Mystici Corporis" in which he outlined the foundations of Christian community, the Body of Christ.

When we look back and see that great burst of phallic energy in the Second Vatican Council, recall the great enthusiasm we all experienced as we looked forward to a renewed Church. But what happened to that energy? It was quickly encircled by a number of powerful, but fearful men, who because they did not know themselves as men, could not trust the Council, the Bishops, much less the people out there, to carry on the vision; they probably couldn't even trust God to manage this new energy in the Church.

What happened was that it was the religious communities of women who responded to the call of renewal with great energy. Their "receiving" nature allowed them to accept this new life and they knew their role was to nurture it and bring it to birth. When that moment arrived, however, they faced unbelievable obstacles from the "fathers," who should have been ready to embrace the new born energy and lead it to maturity. Like the male lion, who tries to kill the cubs after they are born, so this new life was often snuffed out before it had a chance to grow. The women became anxious, then frustrated, and eventually pretty angry, because their own energy was being diminished, and their hopes for renewal sabotaged. It was not, however, the patriarchal or masculine energies that obfuscated this process, but it was the males of the church, who continued to labor under the need to have everything under control, as though the ordained ministry alone had access to the Holy Spirit.

The vocation problem today is a problem of minus phallic power, minus masculine spirituality. No program, developed by our Bishops or anyone else, using Madison Avenue techniques, is going to produce any vocations in the present state of masculine spirituality, until we address the underlying problem of fatherlessness. When our people, both men and women, are bashing father, ridiculing father, and refusing even to call God, "Father," who would possibly want to enter a ministry that calls one "father?" It is my own opinion here, but I think one of the attractions for some young men, in terms of the seminary or religious community may have been the fact that it was a house of men, a school of and for men, a gathering of men. Although unconsciously, many young men sought life in the seminary or novitiate to find their manhood, or to find that father they did not have. That may have worked some generations back, but I don't think

87

it works today, because when they get to the seminary, instead of finding father, they meet up with Tom, Dick, and Harry – males like themselves still trying to find their own manhood, and trying to discover who they really are. That's not a very healthy situation to be sure.

Both men and women, if not fathered appropriately during their adolescent years, are going to have serious problems in two important areas of life which we have mentioned, namely a problem with their sexuality and a problem with authority. If you are one of those who read the National Catholic Reporter, or any of the more liberal Christian periodicals, these two issues dominate the pages of these magazines or newspapers. They tend to exacerbate the problem by focusing on all of the negative aspects of the issue. Why, we ask? Too often, the folks who write the material cannot be objective, because they are facing the same problems in their own lives and tend to project their own sickness into their writing. Independence is their gospel both as it relates to sexuality and authority. The conservative press, on the other hand, while also focusing on these issues, tends to operate from a sense of dependency. Knowing that these issues are part of who they are, they are relentless in their reliance on external authority. For them it is either black or white. They have a very difficult time working in the gray areas of moral and ethical behavior.

As I continue to study the issue of fatherlessness in our society, it is becoming more and more clear to me, that the solution to the problems that we face today, might well be the recapturing of some sense of biblical authority, even biblical patriarchy. By that I mean, men need to recognize what men's God-given place in the world really is, and that the phallic power or masculine energy, invested in them by the creator, needs to be let loose in the world. Traditionally the battle and the hunt were the places where men found their manhood, where they could exercise their masculine energy, and be their true phallic selves. There are plenty of things to be hunted down in today's world; there are plenty of battles to be fought in the world of society, economics, politics, and yes, spirituality. Every institution, in our culture today, is in desperate need of real masculine energy, exercised by males who have entered into their deep masculine soul. The world needs authentic feminine energy as well – women who have discovered their true feminine spirit. It is the collaboration of the fully developed masculine and feminine working together that will bring back the fathers, bring back the grandfathers, bring back the patriarchs, who will then, in turn, call forth the masculine and the feminine in the men and women of tomorrow.

Masculine spirituality is based on the relationship Jesus had with his Father, our Father. We find this beautifully laid out for us in the Gospel of John. Masculine spirituality is the spirituality of sonship – the "Father and I are one" (John 10:30); or "the Father is in me and I am in him" (John 20:38); "I listen to the Father and I do all that the Father tells me" is the basis for real masculine spirituality: to be a son; to be a father; and to be in the kind of relationship with other men that Jesus had with his Father. Masculine spirituality is a GIVING spirituality – active, doing, aggressive and rational; it is characterized by discipline and commitment. What we have lost, when we have lost the father are: 1) responsibility, 2) accountability, 3) authority, 4) discipline, and 5) obedience. These were qualities in the life of Jesus and of his followers ever since. But without the father, they will not be maintained. Masculine spirituality must also be open to the movements of the Spirit. It should have a touch of adventure about it, even be free to take risks along the way.

When men who possess real masculine energy, who live out an alive spirituality, come to mid-life, and move into the downside of life, their spirituality will take on a more feminine tone: more structure, more regularity, more contemplative, and more subjective. As the fires in the flesh mellow and cool, the passion for God grows. Life's meaning moves from living a devout and apostolic life, to preparing for a holy death, where the male can complete his GIVING by his final surrender to the Father, where "I and the Father will be one" forever. We move from creating life, to enjoying life, to celebrating life. For all of this to happen, brothers, we must retrieve the wild man that is deep within us, discover all of the phallic qualities of manhood, and regain and recreate a new world, where men do their God-given thing and women do their God-given thing, and both together are renewing the face of the earth. That, of course, is and will be the work of the Holy Spirit in both.

What we really need to do is focus our attention much more on a new direction for our lives as men, as males, as sons, and as fathers. We want to recapture the biblical image and begin living it out in our own circumstances wherever we happen to find ourselves today. We need to move in a three-fold direction: first, to make ourselves aware of the situation we find ourselves in now. Once we bring this reality to consciousness, then it need not control us any longer. To ignore it and pretend it doesn't exist, is to give it control over us.

Secondly, to turn to the great Healer, Jesus the Lord, submit our broken masculinity to his healing love, and if necessary even employ the assistance of a counselor or spiritual director.

Thirdly, to put into practice in our own lives, clearly defined and understood masculine roles, especially where we are in a family situation. One of the most important male roles is in the area of spiritual leadership. In spite of what we hear from our feminist sisters about male domination, the spiritual life for the last two hundred years has been dominated by women. They may not have had any direct power in the areas of politics or business, but they have a power that is far superior and far more influential than any of those so often attributed to men. Thank God, the women moved in; we would be a lot worse off than we are, had they not been willing to do so. However, life in the spirit, is a masculine energy and should be the responsibility of the father. In those situations where the father does take that responsibility seriously, you have much healthier and happier family life. In communities where men are exercising their God-given qualities, one will see power and growth.

In the mid-seventies, a small group of people began a charismatic prayer group at the Cathedral Church where I was the pastor. The group began to grow, and as it did, several men emerged as the leaders. This style of leadership continued for a number of years and soon established itself as a community of pentecostal believers. For some time, over three hundred people met every Tuesday night for prayer, song, teaching and fellowship. Why was this movement so successful when other worthy movements in the church didn't seem to have the same appeal? What the people perceived here was the leadership carried out by strong spiritual men.

What appears to be needed today, not only in our churches but in the world at large, is strong masculine leadership that is rooted in a deep spirituality. There are a multitude of leaders out in the world today, but they don't seem to have the spirituality required for true leadership. Ambition, money, and power appears to be the energy that moves such leadership. All of these, however, are ego-centered, and do not have lasting potential, whereas leadership rooted in a strong spirituality will be concerned for the common good of all.

SIGNS OF HOPE

Rick from the capital city and his four hopes for the future.

Brian and his teenage sons offer hope in the Big Sky country.

Ernie, a realtor and great cook with his twin sons, now in college. Yes, there is hope in the upper Gallatin.

YES, THERE IS HOPE

Throughout the pages of this manuscript, and discussing these critical issues that confront men (and women) today, there may be a temptation to despair and despondency. Some years ago, I read in one of the local newspapers a startling fact: both the Mayor and Chief of Police in Houston, Texas were women. Houston is one of the largest cities in America, and I am asked to believe that there are no men in Houston who can tackle the job of city leadership and city policing? I don't think this is just a question of equality for women. This is just another form of oppression, forcing women to do men's jobs because the men are either incapable or unwilling to fulfill the roles that they have been created to do.

The question that continues to nag us is: Is there any hope? Can this downward spiraling be arrested? Can we find ways to rescue men from this sickness that afflicts the world? If we look at the situation purely from a sociological point of view, then yes, it is very hopeless indeed. This hopelessness seems to be energized by the reports coming out of the Middle East, where there seems to be no end to the violence there. Where are the real men who can confront the futility of such an approach to the problems they face there? One wonders whether the men there are fervent Muslims, or whether Islam even has a spiritual answer to their angst?

As Christians we have to look at it from a different perspective. From a theological perspective there is, of course, hope. Don't we see this in the account of Jesus' disciples after the passion, death, and burial of Jesus? They were devastated by what had happened to their leader, but they still had hope. In the deep recesses of their memories, there was that promise of Jesus: "And on the third day I will rise again." (Matt. 16:21) Yes, there was hope!

In every age, strong and creative men seem to emerge to rescue the family, the society or the Church. God is not going to allow us to destroy ourselves, unless, of course, that is in his own plan for us. I don't think it is. Solutions, however, need to be drastic, because the illness is so far advanced. The solutions that come to mind for me are: 1) Awareness of the truth of a sick situation is the first step to recovery or healing, and that is the purpose of this manuscript; 2) Conversion to Jesus Christ and his Gospel together with prayer; 3) Long-term counseling and psychotherapy with inner healing. We look at it with the eyes of hope. Yes, there are things we can do that will give some direction to a recovery process.

The first step, as already mentioned, to any healing process is AWARENESS. We have to be made conscious, both as individuals, and as a society that we have a problem here. We have to accept this problem and try to understand the nature of it. Where did it come from and what are the consequences, if we do nothing about it? My hope is that this book, along with others that I have cited in this work, may be the first steps to raise consciousness to the reality of the problem by outlining the origins of the problem, and pointing to some ramifications and consequences that may yet lie ahead.

Next is PRAYER, since the seriousness of the issue and the extent of the consequences all tie in with the spiritual nature of man. Because the pathology seems to be so advanced, only in cooperation with God can we ever hope to achieve any success in the healing process. Pray for yourselves, pray for the men in your life: your own father, your own sons, and your grandsons. Pray for the men who have been called to leadership in the state and in the church. We also need to encourage our men to be men of prayer. In this connection, Christian conversion has proven to be a powerful source of healing for unfathered fathers.

And finally, the third step is PSYCHOTHERAPY together with counseling and inner healing. Once we recognize the nature and depth of our problem we must be willing to take the risk to undertake some pretty drastic kinds of treatment. Recall the steps that Dr. Hardenbrook suggests in his book, particularly as it pertains to your own personal lives.

Most of these will parallel what we discover in the Promise Keeper movement as well as in John Eldridge's retreats and also in the Cursillo movement.

Commitment. For any program to be successful, the men will need to make a serious commitment: first, to real fatherhood, and then to the program itself, whichever one they choose. They must also take the lead not only in restoring stability to their own home, but also, together with their brothers, bring peace to the dysfunctional homes in their own neighborhood and community; secondly, Christian men must commit themselves to the care and guidance of God, the Father. Jesus is our model here. It will be a long and often times a painful journey.

Models. As pointed out elsewhere, boys need fathers who are committed to provide good example to their sons. This means they must not only be successful in their chosen occupation or professions, but equally successful in living godly lives, and being a real spiritual leader in their household. This means he must work at becoming a man of virtue, which word comes to us from the Latin VIR, meaning man, thus to say manly strength.

A Man of Principle. Men, especially fathers, must commit themselves to principle. They need to learn principles, whether from the Scriptures, the teachings of the church, or from spiritual counselors. Fathers have to be firm in applying these principles to family life, to say "no" with both feet planted firmly on the ground, and be courageous in saying "no" to things, bad or good, that would compromise the spiritual health of the family. America needs such men today: family men, men who worship God, and men who are respectful of their Christian brothers and sisters, because they have been created in his image.

Brotherhood. *Men need other men for support and growth. Healthy comradeship is important in teaching and reminding men about who they are. This "time with the boys" is not an escape from, or substitute for, family responsibility, but a supportive change of scene that renews his own sense of manhood and fatherhood.* [6]

In the end, all of this suggests that men must be willing to see the demons in their lives, particularly that of selfish independence. We need to recognize that becoming a responsible father doesn't mean that you enter into some kind of dependency that will entrap you; rather, it is a question of interdependence, the surrendering and receiving from your wife and children, the love, the care, the support, the correction, and the challenge, any and all of which are essential in any relationship. The male in the family is called to be the great "giver," the one who truly sacrifices himself for the life and health of the family. The most important gift you give to your family is your love, expressed both in word and in deeds. Do not be afraid to tell your wife and your children, boys and girls, that you love them. Words are not enough! Let those verbal expressions of love be authenticated by loving attitudes and actions.

---

6   Hardenbrook's <u>Missing in Action</u>

MEN'S MOVEMENTS

Throughout the years that I have been involved in this ministry to men, I have responded to, or investigated different movements that seemed to offer some hope for the healing of broken manhood. Soon after Robert Bly wrote his book, "Iron John," several programs were designed to meet the need explored by Bly in this book. Most of these were psychological and secular in tone. The spiritual or faith dimension seemed to be missing in them. From my Christian bias, I knew they couldn't work over the long haul. Alcoholics Anonymous recognized this early on, and although they tried to avoid any specific faith expression, they would speak of "your higher power" which plays an important role in the healing process of that particular brokenness.

PROMISE KEEPERS

Somewhere in the mid 1990's, I was introduced to the Promise Keepers movement. This was a grassroots movement founded by Bill McCartney, the former football coach of the University of Colorado at Boulder. This movement was identified by two things. The first being the "Seven Promises:"[7]

> *"A Promise Keeper is committed to:*
>
> *1. Honoring Jesus Christ through worship, prayer, and obedience to God's Word in the power of the Holy Spirit.*

---

7   cf. Seven Promises of Promise Keepers by contributing authors, Focus on the Family Press

2. *Pursuing vital relationships with a few other men, understanding that he needs brothers to help him keep his promises.*

3. *Practicing spiritual, moral, ethical and sexual purity.*

4. *Building strong marriages and families through love, protection and biblical values.*

5. *Supporting the mission of his church by honoring and praying for his pastor, and by actively giving his time and resources.*

6. *Reaching beyond any racial and denominational barriers to demonstrate the power of biblical unity.*

7. *Influencing his world, being obedient to the Great Commandment and the Great Commission."*

Secondly, by the large scale "rallies" held all over the country. Thousands of men would come together for a weekend of prayer, teaching, and fellowship. Outstanding teachers and preachers would be invited to speak or preach to the men. Most of the men were from Protestant evangelical communions. Encouraged to do so, by some of our Cursillo brothers, I attended a number of the regional conferences. Although there is still a national organization, and the large conferences continue to be scheduled, the local presence has ebbed considerably. In my opinion, the leadership at the national and local levels didn't put enough emphasis on the importance of prayer and sharing for the small weekly gathering of men. Many, however, often speak of the rally as a turning point in their lives, and they continue to be influenced by it, both in their relationship with their spouses and children, and in their various church communities.

CURSILLO

We learned in the Cursillo movement that it is in the fidelity to the small group gathering, where the strength of the movement lies; it is here that real growth can occur. This movement originated in Spain in the late 1950's. The church there had been devastated by the horrors of a long civil war. The Bishops turned to laymen to develop Christian leadership, not just in the church, but in all the environments where they functioned. It spread from diocese to diocese, and became a powerful tool for the church to reclaim the Spanish people. Soon the movement began spreading elsewhere. It came to our country through the help of some Air Force personnel, who had been stationed in Spain. Originally, the Cursillo was used as a tool to enliven the faith of the Hispanic community in the southwest. Today, I would surmise that there are Cursillo programs in every one of the Roman Catholic dioceses here in the United States. Parallel versions have since appeared in other churches: "Walk to Emmaus" in the United Methodist; "Koinonia" in the Lutheran; and "Pathways" in the Episcopal. Each of these have adapted the program according to their own theological and liturgical tradition.

The original purpose of leadership and environmental changes continues to be the focus of the dynamic of the weekend. Along side of that, it became evangelistic, as more and more men who signed up for the weekend did not have a personal relationship to his God.

Then, in recent years, it has become a tool for re-fathering and healing. Since more and more men today suffer from this absent father syndrome, it is here in this program that they seem to retrieve or recover their manhood just from the love, the concern, and the challenge given them by the men on the team. Then they are encouraged and challenged to continue the graces of the weekend by forming small prayer groups of five or six men, who meet once a week for an hour, to pray and to share how their faith walk is going.

RANSOMED HEART MINISTRIES

One of the more successful programs, addressing this issue is a ministry created by the work of John Eldridge, who, at the end of the last century began publishing a series of books that was focused on this very issue we have been discussing, namely, the loss of manhood, and the absence of father and fathering in our culture. John didn't just write about it, he first established himself in a brotherhood of Christian men, and together they created a retreat format into which men were invited to share their stories. This was eventually published on a DVD disc and made available to others. We took advantage of this in 2003, and offered the program to forty-two of our Cursillo men which, in my judgment, was well received and provided some real challenges for their lives. Later, I formed a team of a few of these men, and we offered the program to men in other parishes in our area, again with considerable success. Of all the programs or ministries out there, this one has reached thousands and thousands of men all over the country, and today is being offered abroad as well. Because of the strong emphasis on a strong group of brothers, this movement has, in fact, provided healing purpose for many of our brothers in this country and abroad. Here is a real sign of hope for the men of the world and their beleaguered families.

In his latest book, John Eldridge seems to have felt called to go even deeper into the spiritual aspects of his project. In that book, "The Way of the Wild Heart," he stresses the importance of the Father-God relationship. God is always there and available to heal the brokenness and suffering occasioned by the fatherless syndrome. I personally know of situations where the conversion of a father became, not only a closer relationship with his Lord, but also the healing of those psychic deficits, which were the result of the dysfunction in his relationship with his biological father. As a result, these men have become great fathers to their own sons and daughters.

When I was the director of our Diocesan Retreat Center, I became acquainted with a spirit-filled couple who were involved in a number of apostolic movements in the church: marriage encounter, charismatic renewal, and children's ministry. Bob, the father in this situation, came to healing of his own "father wound" through marriage encounter where he opened up to a relationship with God, our Father. He not only became a good father for his own growing brood, but he fathered the local prayer group for many years, and with the aid of his energetic spouse, fathered retreat ministries for teenagers.

Another example, where God became the father he needed, was a man I met recently who told me his story. He was adopted and although his adoptive father was good to him, there was that emptiness in his heart that needed healing. When he looked back on his life he confessed that early on he felt that there was someone out there looking after him. This feeling developed into a relationship with God as the Father he needed. As a result he was able to father and shepherd a large family in the ways of the Lord.

One might say, when all else fails, God is always there to come to the rescue.

In a Father's Day issue of Johnny Hart's comic strip, B.C., the old guru is sitting under a tree writing these lines by John Wiley:

> *"A day is as a thousand years.*
> *Everybody don't all have a father.*
> *Some there are whose dads have passed along.*
> *Then there's some who couldn't give less bother,*
> *to family situations woe begone.*
> *With dads you cannot just reach out and nab one*
> *to pull the family out of its despair,*
> *if for some reason you don't have one*
> *there's one on duty all the time– up there!"*

REFLECTION VIII

RITUALS OF INITIATION OR PASSAGE RITES

As we continue in this effort to understand all that goes on in the life of a boy, physically, intellectually, emotionally, and spiritually, it will be to our advantage to see how one moves from one stage to another. This "how" we call the rite of passage or rituals of initiation. Moore and Gillette in their book on the masculine archetypes, suggest that a *"man who cannot get it together is a man who probably has not had the opportunity to undergo ritual initiation into the deep structures of manhood. He remains a boy – not because he wants to, but because no one has shown him the way to transform his boy energies into man energies."*[8]

One of the evils we inherited from the industrial revolution was the loss of the father-son relationship, and the ways in which manhood was passed on from one generation to the next. In the pre-industrial era, there were no particular rites that were employed to initiate a young boy into manhood, but there were passage moments or events, as it were – inviting his son to take the reins of his team and drive the wagon home; or turning over the tractor ordering him to plow the lower forty. The message he got was, "My father is trusting me to do a man's job!" The boys worked side-by-side with their fathers often from dawn 'til dusk. They absorbed much of who and what their father was.

Along with Moore & Gillette, Robert Bly, Richard Rohr, John Eldridge, and other authors I have read on

---

8   Moore, R., & Gillette, D., "Warrior, King, Magician, Lover"

manhood, all speak of the role of initiatory rites or moments as both important and necessary, if we are to recover the values and performance of real manhood in our current culture. Unlike "bar-mitzvah," which is the coming of age of Jewish males with a meaningful rite and celebration, the vision of an appropriate rite must be one of a process, which has its high points at each stage.

Jesus, no doubt experienced the Bar-mitzvah ritual when he was thirteen, with Joseph and Mary playing the normal Jewish parental roles. The sole scriptural evidence of his teen age years was his escapade in the temple.

Recall the scene at the Jordan, when John is approached by Jesus for his baptismal rite. We are told of the dove that hovers over him, indicating the presence of that anointment of the Spirit; we hear the Father's powerful voice: "You are my beloved Son in whom I am well pleased!" (Luke 3:22) Jesus now passes from the comfort and security of that modest home in Nazareth, to his assigned ministry, for which he prepares by his long fasting experience in the desert.

A similar moment took place on Mt. Tabor where Jesus is transfigured before his friends, and again we hear the Father, "This is my beloved Son. Listen to him." This Transfiguration experience was most important to the early Christians, as it appears in all of the synoptic Gospels. (Matt. 17:5; Mark 9:7; Luke 9;35) We might view this as the passage from ministry to suffering. In the garden of Gethsemane another passage, from his will into the Father's will, was experienced in the horrors of his passion and death.

These were all significant moments in the life of Jesus, the man. We don't have much in the gospels to accent the movement from one stage of masculine growth to another, as we have outlined it. We note his adolescent escapade in Jerusalem, where he is finally located in the temple chatting with the elders there. He certainly had many warrior experiences as he was challenged by Satan in the desert; or accused of blasphemy by the scribes and Pharisees; he battled also against a wide range of sickness and disease; physical, emotional, and spiritual. But he was also a great King archetype, for wherever he went and whatever he did, there was no doubt as to who was central at the moment.

So we see in the life of Jesus the importance of these special moments, when a man moves from one stage or archetype to the next. It's not that he leaves one behind and absorbs completely the next. No! There will always be a crossing over, a blending, that continues throughout the life cycle. Events or circumstances will dictate the kind of archetypal energy needed to resolve an issue. In one case, you may need to be on top of it as leader and director; in another, you may have to get into the muck and mire with your warrior energy. On other occasions the wisdom of the magician may be the energy required, or even the compassion and caring of the lover may be what is needed. In some cases, you may be blending several of these energies to apply to a given desperate situation.

In my own case, I do not recall any significant passage rite or event suggesting that I would be entering the man's world. When I was in the seventh grade, I was prepared for the Sacrament of Confirmation where the Bishop would lay hands on me and anoint me with the oil of chrism, making me, as the instructions indicated, "a strong and perfect Christian and a soldier of Jesus Christ." Looking back on this moment, with the blessing of hindsight, I can see that perhaps the Church, or at least those responsible for our formation at the time, missed a really important opportunity to expand the implications in the terms we have been discussing.

More recently, it would seem that we are not supposed to even mention the "soldier of Jesus Christ." The attitude implied by this forgets that we are still in a battle, and we still need soldiers in the realm of the spirit, where the real war continues to go on.

Returning to my own case, perhaps I sensed a movement from boyhood to manhood when my father allowed me to drive the car, even by myself, at the age of fourteen. Interestingly, my mother ceased driving once I was able to do the driving for her. There were two "men" in the family now who did all the driving and whatever chauffeuring needed to be done. When the United States entered the Second World War, my father volunteered for the Sea Bees and was sent off to Alaska to do construction work on the Aleutian Islands. Since my mother didn't drive, it was suggested that I take the family car to college. Looking back on this now, I am not so sure that I was the focus of this decision, but rather my younger brother, who was now in his teens, and my mother did not want to deal with the issues that would arise if the car was at home. Anyway, I arrived at Carroll College with our car, the only student with a car, which was pretty unique at that time. However, I was promptly relieved of the keys to that car by the Dean of Men. On occasions when there was a real need, the Dean would kindly return the keys.

Fred and his two warrior sons armored for the battle...
Yes, there is hope in Alabama.

THE ROLE OF SPORTS

Athletic activities and sporting games offer occasions and opportunities for the warrior archetype to emerge in a boy's life. By his participation in competitive games, he hones the masculine qualities of aggression, creativity, and endurance. During my own educational years, sports was not the over-riding element in schooling that it is today. Yes, there was an emphasis on fair play and sportsmanship, and yes, each team longed to be the winner, and played hard to achieve the victory. But everybody knew that there are also losers and the need to be trained in a way by which that eventuality would be gracefully accepted. In those days "winning" wasn't the only thing. Just as important were attitude, sportsmanship, and the skill in playing the game.

However, there seems to be so much out there in the world of sports that militates against a kindly view of this topic. What has been happening in the world of athletic competition in recent years appears to reveal that all too many athletes, even among the pros, have not left the adolescent stage yet. It is important, therefore, that we do this reflection because all that has been occurring lately in the field of professional sports does effect the masculine journey we are discussing in this work.

As I write these lines the famous "Tour de France" is coming to the conclusion of its 2007 race, which has been devastated by a series of cheating scandals. This has been the premier athletic event in France for over one hundred years and has gained popularity and participation from all over the world.

Coupled with this misfortune are the scandals surrounding all of the major pro sports in this country. Manhood has been taking a beating in all of this. What is going on here, in my view, is an application of the current cultural values to the world of sports. Our culture has shifted the central focus of sports from the "love of the game" to an obsession for winning, especially if there is money involved.

Because sports often provides the time and place for boys to develop some of their masculine qualities, as well as occasions for fathers and sons to interrelate, I feel it appropriate to research even the history of sports and games. My inspiration for this comes from a little book by Thomas Ryan entitled, "Wellness, Spirituality and Sports." In his book, Ryan provides some insight into the meaning and history of this topic, by introducing the reader to a classic work on this subject, "Homo Ludens: A Study of the Play Element in Culture" by John Huizinga.

In this interesting work we discover that games and sports, in the earliest records of their presence in the human history, were generally associated with religious or social festivals. Such sporting activities did not include organized teams or groups, but more likely the competition between two individual athletes, such as the field events that we see in current track meets. Even the original Olympic Games were a collection of one-on-one sports. The competition between teams of players is a modern addition to the Olympics.

The view of athletics as important cultural values did not appear until the end of the eighteenth century. By the end of the following century, games and sports were taken more seriously. More structured team competition began to emerge and there were now elaborate and strict rules. At this point the keeping of records was established. However, as these changes continued to develop, it began to spill over into the more sedentary games such as chess, backgammon, and a variety of card games.

What happened, as a result of all this systematization of sports was the unholy loss of the spirit of fun and enjoyment. Since sports was transformed into big business as we see it today, it has completely lost the play-fun factor. For the modern professional athlete, sports is a job, a work, a living, and this attitude is beginning to trickle down into our college sporting programs.

In the world of sports today we are operating on the maxim "winning at any cost." This attitude robs sports of its fundamental and traditional purposes: healthy play, sportsmanship, entertainment. Today it is all about "winning" and "money." Even the gambling world has invaded the sports arena and not for the good of the game either.

Let us get back to the values of sports for growing boys, and the place it can have in the development of manhood. It can also provide occasion for a "passage rite." From a number of interviews I have been able to conduct, I discovered that sporting contests are ideal situations for this to occur, but it is also a wonderfully healthy time for fathers and sons to develop their own relationship. It can be a time for "wounding" as well. In this world of "winning is everything," over zealous dads can make unreal demands on a young athlete's performance. When the boy doesn't measure up, and Dad berates him or humiliates him before his peers, he will inflict a deep wound in the heart of his son. One father told me his story that exemplifies this. He had the misfortune of playing in a little league team whose coach was his own father. As the pitcher in the game, he wasn't doing too well and this frustrated the father-coach, prompting him to shout "if that's the best you can do, maybe we should get one of the cheerleaders to do it for you." This was a pain that this youngster carried with him long into his adult life. Fortunately, it did get resolved and eventually forgiveness and healing took place. But this "woundedness" is often not recognized and can continue to have very negative effects on his later life, and on his relationship with his father.

On the other hand, I know fathers who tend to put a positive twist on a son's athletic performance. "I know, son, you really did the best you could, but WE are going to work on those baskets, aren't we?" Notice the word "we" here. Improvement in performance is going to be a joint effort in which dad will be a part. Bonding can be achieved without any wounds. The son here knows the concern and love that his father has for him. He knows that he is a beloved son.

I conclude this reflection with some thoughts again inspired by Moore and Gillette. This crisis of failing manhood is very much a reality in our world today, simply because we have no healthy models to emulate, and no initiatory events or processes to inspire the young male to access those manly qualities and virtues needed for healthy manhood. The sins and crimes of the professional athlete are spread in glaring headlines across both the printed press and the media, while at the same time the virtues and noble achievements of their peers are left unreported and unseen by the emerging athlete. He is presented a vision of what is worst in an athlete, and deprived of what is best. Thus, many fall by the wayside and rarely reach that level of male maturing where he can say, "I am a man today!"

Secondly, there is the absence of initiatory rites or events simply because there are no fathers to employ them for their sons. As a result, boys too often turn to what is called pseudo-rites, such as we have seen in inner city "gangs." For a young boy to be fathered into manhood, the environment for this journey must be created and managed by men, for only men can lead boys into manhood. What the current culture today desperately needs is the recovery of these rites for the men-to-be of tomorrow. In a fatherless society this will be hard to achieve.

There is hope in Illinois
with John and his Sons,
here relaxing in Hawaii.

REFLECTION IX

THE MASCULINE JOURNEY

We now return to a theme we began with in the onset of this work, namely, Sonship. You will recall how important that aspect of Jesus' life was. "You are my beloved son in whom I am well pleased." Those were the defining words as Jesus enters into his mission. The baptism in the Jordan, at the hands of John the Baptist, was the backdrop against which these words were spoken, a passage rite, as it were. Jesus now moves from the comfort of his home in Nazareth to the risks and challenges of his ministry. He is now sent out on a forty day retreat in the Judaean desert to prepare for this work.

Before entering into the male journey beyond childhood, there is an important aspect of this picture we must not overlook. And that is the very important role that the mother has in this journey. Her role is foundational, which was pointed out to me in the work by David Heller, "The Soul of a Man." He began this work with several pages about the role of mothers in setting values and mores for sons and daughters from their earliest years, by the way she cared for them. She gives her children the spiritual and social grounding they need as they grow. Mothers provide their children with a sense of their own self image and their self worth, i.e., their personhood. She helps them feel good about themselves. And all of this will be seen as necessary and valuable in all the segments of their journey to adult maturity. As I began this final reflection on manhood, the latest book by John Eldridge became available. I immediately purchased the book and have read it. John seems to have the will to continue to dig ever more deeply into the issues spelled out in my work here. In his work, entitled, "The Way of the Wild Heart," he designs a process by which a boy becomes a man: Son, Cowboy, Warrior, Lover, Sage. He seems to conjoin the archetypal anthropology with his own. I cite this here because there is a striking parallel to what I propose to do as a conclusion to this book, under the rubric of the five "Hoods" – Boyhood, Manhood, Brotherhood, Fatherhood, Sainthood.

In both of these paradigms or models, the essential base is "sonship." As Jesus enters his ministry with the love and praise of his Father, so too, every boy needs to know that he is a beloved Son and that in him his father is well pleased. He longs to hear those words before he can move on in his psychic development. Of course, it does not have to be in these scriptural terms. In fact, it may not have to be in words at all, for the words must come from the sincere heart of the father. It is in the relationship where the heart of the boy knows the heart of the father and that he is beloved.

In the midst of composing this manuscript, I was called to be the spiritual director for a men's Cursillo weekend. At one point in the weekend, several of the men were sharing crises in their lives that involved fourteen-year-old children. This prompted me to use the preaching section of the liturgy to address the issue of fatherhood. Here, I emphasized the tremendous responsibility fathers have toward their sons (and daughters as well). I made an effort to emphasize, as strongly as I could, how boys and girls need to know that they are beloved of their father.

As the son or daughter moves from childhood into adolescence and early adulthood, it is the Father who calls forth from them their manhood or their womanhood. It is the father who names them "man" or "woman." In other words, he gives them gender identity. That is a responsibility that the mother cannot undertake. The mother affirms her child in his or her personhood, his or her dignity as a human being. They need to hear from her "you are my special little one; you are good; you are wonderful."

BOYHOOD

In New Mexico, Zeke and his very young sons bonding with irons no less - Tiger, beware!

As the boy child reaches the use of reason, he becomes aware of two important realities; first, that he is in a safe world because of the presence of that other man that everyone calls "father." He soon discovers that his own relationship to this father person is a source of security and confidence for him. The second reality is that his world is full of mystery and wonder and he must be busy about exploring it.

In this stage, he discovers his own spontaneity and creativity. As a new wonder enters his vision, this must be explored, and so he tends to jump from one activity to another. Along side of this, he also discovers the fun in creating new wonders from the set of Lego blocks, or building sand castles at the beach, followed by the tree house in the family elm or oak, where he also discovers the world of wild animals in the presence of squirrels, raccoons, snakes, and frogs. All of this seems to be achieved without any sense of fear or doubt. Father is always there to help or simply to affirm and approve. And that is very important at this stage, because it is here that the boy comes to know that he is a beloved son.

At this age, I was fortunate that our family lived on a farm, a place replete with mystery, wonder, and adventure. My adventures often ended in disaster, but my sister was always the backup, and would come to the rescue, like the time when I tried to pet a male goose and was promptly attacked. My sister came to the rescue with a supply of the only weapons at hand, rocks, sticks, and dirt with which she forced Mr. Goose to let go of her adventurous brother. Another time my curiosity led me to explore a bee hive, also with an equally devastating outcome. This time my backup took off to the house to seek a rescue operation in the person of my father.

We soon learned that skunks and rattlesnakes were not designed to be house pets and after only one encounter we knew to avoid these interesting creatures. Once again in one of our exploratory ventures, we hiked to our closest neighbor's house to do a little exploration. At that time the basement was accessed by an outside door that needed to be lifted up. With much effort, we managed to open this door to discover a basement flooded with spring water and alive with numerous reptiles. By this time in our young lives we responded by a hasty exit and returned home to safer ground.

It was also during this period that I accompanied my father, as he drove the horses that pulled the drill, planting the seeds for next year's crop. He had seated me behind him on the seed bin, but when the drill bounced across a berm in the freshly plowed field, my dad's passenger fell off the bin and onto the drill bars below. A boy never seems to learn that there is usually a cost for these adventures. Somehow he seems to realize or understand that it is okay. The adventure is worth it.

Somewhere between the boyhood time and the onset of manhood is the period of frenetic growth that we call adolescence, more commonly named "the teen-age years." Physical, intellectual, social, and sexual changes are taking place in the young male and his counterpart, the young female. It is a difficult struggle to keep balance in all of this, to understand the implications of what is going on in one's body and one's mind. It is a very challenging period in the journey. There is a need to go into more depth here, but I'm not that knowledgeable in this area, but I do recognize that this aspect of male development is very critical.

I am aware of a family grouping or clan that has designed a way of bringing teen-agers into manhood. Once a year all the males in the family plan an adventurous outing. At age thirteen or fourteen the younger members of the "clan" are invited to join in the adventure. This ritual seems to be in accord with the process outlined in a book, entitled, "A Fine Young Man" by Michael Gurian, who we are told is a very experienced youth counselor. [9]

---

9   A Fine Young Man by Michael Gurian. He treats all the aspects of adolescent experience, social, biological, and psychological.

For those of this age group, it is a struggle between hanging on to all of the blessings of dependency, and the excitement of moving toward the independence of adulthood. Every boundary set in the family rule book is being challenged at this time. In a well organized family structure, the father now plays his most important role. The father needs to be fully present to his sons at this time, ready to respond to their questions, eager to explain some of the mysteries of life and inter-gender relationships, and anxious to affirm them in their decisions that effect their future well- being. At the same time, mother is not to be ignored. She stands at hand always to support and aid father in his duties at this time. Her feminine instincts and intuition adds greatly to the whole process, as the youngster literally explodes into manhood.

MANHOOD

What does it mean to be a man? This is an important question in this day and age when the secular world has arrayed all of its forces against our manhood. Although not necessarily a new phenomenon in the history of human experience, this recent expression of it is the result of a long process of erosion. Often we look to the modern women's movements as the enemy of manhood. This may be a little simplistic. Men have been involved in that process as well. We have to go deeper into the roots of this phenomenon.

To get at the heart of this issue, John Eldridge, in his writing and ministry, begins with the suggestion that the men come up with a list of their favorite movies, and roles in the movie. They are caught up with the "hero" role in each of these – the story of a real man, who risks all kinds of dangers and enemies to achieve his goal. He is literally a "wild man," but with a brave heart. He moves and operates from his deep spirit, his very soul. This is what is meant when we speak of a man's heart.

In his little book, "The Way of the Heart," Henri Nouwen offers a definition of "heart" that explains for us the meaning of this term, as it is used in this connection. He writes, *". . . the word heart in the Jewish-Christian tradition refers to the source of all physical, emotional, intellectual, volitional, and moral energies. . . . The heart is the central and unifying organ of our personal life. Our heart determines our personality, and is therefore not only the place where God dwells but also the place to which Satan directs his fiercest attacks."*[10]

As we speak of the man's heart, we do not refer to passion and feelings of romantic love. It will include that, and yet goes much deeper into the personality where life's decisions are made, and where contact with the eternal God is discovered. It is this heart of the man that has been destroyed by the secular forces abroad. And it is this heart that we must recover to bring back the authentic manhood as authored by the divine creator.

One of the modern films, that appears on most men's list of favorites is the life story of William Wallace, the hero of the movie "Braveheart," who freed Scotland from oppressive English rule. It was not by chance that Gibson gave this name to this story, for it speaks to the deep heart of a man. This is what I should be: insightful, courageous, daring, and fearless. This may well be the vision of the pre-Eden man as he came forth from the hand of God. And it is that man that we are called to rediscover in these difficult times.

Let us now return to our anthropology for some insights as to what the heart of man would be like. These

10   Henri Nouwen, <u>The Way of the Heart</u> p.77

insights arise out of that unconscious world we described earlier. This focuses on what we call archetypes, elements of manhood displayed in the great epics and tales of the past. John Eldridge focuses on warrior, adventurer, and rescuer of beauty, whereas Robert Bly and Robert Moore focus on those of warrior, king, lover, sage. A number of these archetypes have been downgraded by the culture. They are politically incorrect, as it were. If man has lost his heart through these denials of his basic urges, he will not be able to function as a man in society. He is weakened and deprived of the basic energy that his masculine soul needs to play his role in creation, as the creator intended. He needs a battle to fight; he needs to experience leadership (the king energy); he needs to discover and fight for beauty, wherever he experiences it, whether in the arms of a woman, or in the embrace of nature's awesome wonders. Man needs to express the wisdom gained from a lifetime of battles, adventures, and loving, and pass it on to the next generation. These archetypes define his manliness, his gender. They are his heart.

Recovering the heart of one's manhood is a high priority journey, to say the least. We need a battle to fight, but that doesn't mean we pick a fight every time we go to a bar; or that we enlist in the armed forces. What this means is that we are called to enter that battle in the realm of the Spirit, and equip ourselves to do battle in behalf of justice and truth. A doctor is in the battle against disease and pain; a social worker is in the war against hunger and poverty; a lawyer is in the battle against injustice and lawlessness. Where are the men that should be standing against the evils prevalent in society today, especially in the world of education and the world of politics? Who is doing battle for God's side in these areas?

The cultural agenda for the restoration of society must include the healing of the masculine heart. Men and women need to understand what it is that God, or nature if you wish, has given to each gender all that makes them to be who they are in his eyes. Adam is not Eve; and Eve is not Adam; but together they image God to the world, and they share his creative power. For that to work, however, man must be fully masculine and woman must be fully feminine.

The fully alive image of masculinity, and the fully alive image of femininity was corrupted and shattered by what happened in Eden, as described for us in the Book of Genesis. It is that fully alive image that we need to recover. How can we do that, you will ask? That is the reason Jesus came into the world – to rescue each of us from our disunity, to make right all the disorder caused by sin, to heal the dysfunction in our lives and our relationships.

Recall the words of the Prophet Isaiah, which Jesus quotes as he begins his ministry: *"The Spirit of the Lord is upon me, because he has anointed me to bring glad tidings to the poor. He has sent me to proclaim liberty to captives and recovery of sight to the blind, to let the oppressed go free, and to proclaim a year acceptable to the Lord!"* (Luke 4:18-19)

Too often we see his mission only in sociological terms, but he is talking about the war going on within the spirit of every man, woman, and child. He has come to "heal the broken hearted and set them free...to give sight to the spiritually blind . . . to release those in the captivity of sin . . .to lift up those oppressed by fear and guilt. Yes, there was a sociological dimension to this prophecy and Jesus used it generously as a sign or a witness to his divinity and to his mission as well. What he was really addressing was the power invested in him by that Spirit, to bring healing and unity to the spiritual brokenness and the spiritual dysfunction in the children of God, who were corrupted by the consequences of the sin of our first parents.

In his book, "The Joy of Priesthood," Fr. Rossetti concludes his section on "the Priest as a male" with this summation, *"Within this cultural bias against masculinity and maleness, the priest as a man must be courageous enough to welcome his masculinity, embrace it, and express it in a balanced way. This might be difficult in this climate, but it is nonetheless one of his tasks. Ironically, the priest who is not able to embrace his masculinity in a positive way is prone to lapsing into one of two destructive extremes. He may either repress his masculinity and become 'wishy-washy' and indecisive, feeling guilty and apologizing for his maleness, or he may fall into the other extreme, becoming aggressive, power hungry, and domineering.*

Becoming a mature male means being comfortable with one's masculinity and thus not needing to hide it or exaggerate it. We ought not apologize for being a man. At the same time we ought not use our masculinity as a weapon."[11]

Manhood was described powerfully in the well-known poem of Rudyard Kipling, "IF." Here are some of the lines excerpted for this purpose:

If you can keep your head when all about you
are losing theirs and blaming it on you,
If you can trust yourself when all men doubt you
but make allowance for their doubting too
Or being lied about, don't deal in lies
Or being hated, don't give way to hating,
And yet don't look too good, or talk too wise.
". . . if you can meet with Triumph or Disaster
and treat those two impostors just the same,
If you can bear to hear the truth you've spoken
Twisted by knaves to make a trap for fools,
Or watch the things you gave your life to, broken

11   [9]The Joy of Priesthood, Stephen Rossetti, p.104

And stoop and build 'em up with worn-out tools.
". . .If you can talk with crowds and keep your virtue
or walk with kings - nor lose the common touch
If neither foes nor loving friends can hurt you;
If all men count with you, but none too much,
If you can fill the unforgiving minute
With sixty seconds' worth of distance run,
Yours is the Earth and everything that's in it,
And - which is more - you'll be a man, my son!

Manhood, then, is not achieved easily, it comes only with much struggle and hard work, crossing many wobbly bridges, climbing many difficult crags. It takes will power and courage along each step of the journey. We are losing our men today because they have been taught the easy way, avoiding all the necessary, but inconvenient, steps that must be taken to acquire that precious gift of manliness.

BROTHERHOOD

This brotherhood meets for prayer and sharing
every Friday at 6:00 a.m.
Yes, there is Hope in the Gallatin Valley.

In this important search for the true masculine, the seeker soon discovers that this is an enterprise he cannot do alone. Because it is difficult and challenging, he needs the aid and support of other men. Manhood is conveyed or passed down by men and it is maintained and supported by men.

In the movie, "Braveheart," William Wallace's manhood was passed on by a great father, but it was strengthened and supported by his followers; D'Artagnan, who also had a great father, would never have survived without the companionship of the other Muskateers; Lewis and Clark succeeded in their battle with a hostile environment only with the support and aid of the "Corps of Discovery;" Ernest Shakelton, on his famous sail to the Antarctic with all of its difficulties, managed to bring his support group through it all with not the loss of a single brother. Another example which comes to mind is the J.R.R.Tolkien trilogy, the Lord of the Rings. Frodo would never have accomplished his mission without the aid of the fellowship.

Even Jesus' own mission was abetted and supported by those loyal disciples; we could go on and on with examples throughout history and literature, to evidence this need that men have for other men in their lives.

The founders of all of the great religious orders were in battle array against the evils of their time, by surrounding themselves with like-spirited men. Francis, against the greed and opulence of his time; Dominic, against the heresies and ignorance of his time; Vincent de Paul, against the poverty and hunger of Paris; John Bosco, against the juvenile crime on the streets of Rome. Each, in turn, needed other men to keep those fires going in their hearts.

All too often wives will bemoan some of the social activities in which their men engage, because it takes them out of the home. And yet there is a need for the Saturday morning golf foursome; the poker game at Mike's; the quick stop at Pat's saloon for a quaff of beer with the fellas on the way home. These are all a part of the pattern - man's need for the society of men. If they abuse this, as sometimes they do, by becoming addicted to them to the detriment of family, and of themselves, they perhaps have not yet advanced from the adolescent stage.

FATHERHOOD

In this progression of the masculine journey I have designed here, Fatherhood is at the apex of the male story. If he knows that he is the beloved of the father; if he has weathered the ambivalence of teendom; and if he has entered the world of manhood, he is now ready for the next stage. Hopefully, he will be equipped with all the talents and skills he will need for a deeper level of relationship, which will be an intimate association with his lady fair through courtship, engagement, marriage, and offspring.

Fatherhood, in the Christian tradition, is the pinnacle of a man's relationship with women, for from their number he now is moved to choose his beloved, his beauty, soon at the altar and then in the bed. Fatherhood presumes marriage and sex here. There are so many aspects of our secular society today that are inimical to fatherhood, even to marriage itself. There seems to be a concerted effort to undermine this deep-seated longing in the male heart. The whole focus of the marital relationship has been turned up side down. It was for that very reason I thought it necessary and important to address the subject of sex in this book, with the hope that it would give us a better understanding of the current chaos we are experiencing in this moment of the history of the human race.

Whether a man marries or not, he is always hard-wired for progeny, for within the depths of his masculine heart is that desire for sons and/or daughters. Fatherhood is not necessarily limited to marriage. There are many avenues for the man to pursue and fulfill that longing in his heart. The educational world affords many opportunities for single men, or men from fruitless marriages, to practice "fathering" as teachers, coaches, or counselors. Boy Scouting or Little League sports are venues where boys can be guided and formed. For boys and girls coming from fatherless homes, this can be a crucial role that men in these positions can offer, which the children's own father was not available to do. Here, the young man can become the beloved son; here, he can experience the values of authentic manhood to be emulated in his own journey. We are all aware of well-known athletes, who have witnessed to their own conversion through the ministry of a coach, a recruiter, or teacher. What a wonderful way to break the cycle of bad fathering, and offer to a new generation values and attitudes that will set them on the right track to become the men and fathers of tomorrow.

I came upon a film when I was working on the "Wild at Heart Retreats" entitled simply "The Kid." I choose to rename it "The Tale of Two Fathers." The story focuses entirely on a boy's dream to be a great boxer. But in the process of the story, it exemplifies all that is worst in poor fathering. The father of the boy with the dream is totally uninvolved in his son's dream. He won't even listen. His opposition is adamant and unrelenting, which forces the young boy to pursue his dream in circuitous and dishonest ways. That father has placed his son in the untenable dilemma of choosing between his love for his father and his love for his dream.

At the other end of the story this boy, "the kid," whose name is Jimmy, has a close friend, Russ, who is also in the boxing program. His father is too involved because he is imposing his own dream on his son. This boy has no love for this sport at all.

Now enters the surrogate father(s). Rod Steiger plays the role of Harry, a one time national boxing champ, who now in his declining years runs a gym program for inner city boys with the help of an African-American trainer. These two men are supplying the kind of fathering for these kids that is missing in their own homes. They tend to usher these boys through a very important stage of their masculine development, where fathering is so critical to their future well being.

For surrogate fathers, there is an important caution. In the light of all the frenzy, over the abuse and molestation of children in all kinds of situations, one must approach their relationships with young people at this time, with great care. One must be very circumspect about how he or she expresses their interest and care for such needy children. Touching, caressing, or patting is no longer a proper method of showing your concern and your support.

One of the targets of the feminist movement, long before the Boston scandal, was the Catholic priesthood and its long standing tradition of calling their ordained celibate ministers "Father." That famous quote from Jesus in the gospels where he says, "call no man father..." was used to suggest that priests should not be addressed in this way. When one looks at the role of the priest, at least in the church, one can see that his ministry is also open to fathering possibilities. He fathers the spiritual journey of the flock through Baptism, Confirmation, Eucharist and Reconciliation, as well as in Matrimony and the Anointing of the Sick. Here he is present to the believer as a true father, the author of life in the Spirit in each sacramental occasion. He may not be worthy to be so addressed, but his role in the spiritual order almost demands this recognition. The whole concept of priesthood, the mediator between God and his people, suggests that the "Fatherhood" of

God is symbolized in the flesh by the "fatherhood" of his ministers.

In my own case, having been ordained to the priesthood in times ancient, it was a predetermined given that this young man of twenty-five years would be, from then on "father!" Even in my own family, males and females alike began addressing me as father. My own father particularly, and not a Roman Catholic, to the day of his death always called me "father," likewise, my brothers to this day, always address me in this way. All of this, in the beginning, was embarrassing and awkward, but eventually it became a source of great humbling. This should not imply that this is the way it should be, but what it does say is that was a generation that had great respect for the role of fatherhood, no matter where and how it was exercised.

Effective fathering is so crucial to the proper functioning of society, and as we have noted throughout this work, fathering is in short supply. The reason for this is a matrix of social pressures and demands that prevents authentic manhood, the prerequisite for good fathering.

Brian at his wedding with his father, Jim, and his six brothers. A great hope in Penn-sylvania

SAINTHOOD

We have journeyed through the various aspects of what it means to be a man. We now come to the last segment of that journey. Like the alpine climber, we are struggling in the final pitch to reach the goal which he has desired all the time. In the end of our own journey, we know that deep within the masculine soul there is that desire for the mountain top experience, namely to be as close to God as possible . . . to be a saint.

We began these reflections with the "Call to Holiness." That is the call of the gospel itself; it was the call of Vatican II; and it was the call of Pope John Paul II. Over and over again, we are reminded that as creatures of our heavenly Father, each one has indeed been given that basic vocation, namely, to be holy, to be perfect, to be a saint.

By the Sacrament of Baptism, reinforced by that of Confirmation, we are called to become a saint. That was and is our vocation! There are two things we have to keep in mind as we continue our journey through all of these phases: first, we will not achieve that goal on our own in this life, but we will put forth as much effort as we can to measure up to the challenge, relying always on the presence and guidance of the Holy Spirit of God. Secondly, we have no means to measure our holiness. All we can do is respond to the guidelines offered through the Word of God and the Body of Christ, the Church.

Actually, the only concrete measurement is how we stack up against the witness and testimony of the many saints in the tradition. It is always helpful, and a means of encouragement, to read the lives of great men and women of the past who have been set forth as models of holiness and perfection.

Here I offer an example in the life and ministry of Frederic Ozanam, the founder of the St. Vincent de Paul Society, recently beatified by Pope John Paul II. His life provides a model of what it means to listen to the Spirit, and do God's will in all things – to be a man with a man's heart.

Only forty years old when he died, but in that forty years he made the journey we have been talking about in full strides. He came into the world sickly, having almost died of typhoid fever when he was seven. He had, however, two major advantages: first, his father was a physician; secondly, his parents were devout Catholics in a France that had turned its back on the church and religion. Frederic's father, for example, was not reluctant to make house calls, and often, after treating the patient medically, would kneel at his bed side and pray for the sick person. His mother was the head of a group called the "Night Watchers," who provided nighttime, at home, nursing care for the poor. What an environment to grow up in! In spite of his fragile health he set high goals and standards for himself. At thirteen, he began to write prose and poetry in both French and Latin. By seventeen, he was fluent in Latin and Greek and often conversed with his father in Latin. Later, he even became facile in German, English, Hebrew and Sanskrit.

As a consequence of his interest in philosophy and theology, he entered into a period of doubt and depression about his faith. It was a great time of struggle for him that lasted throughout one whole year. However, he managed to rise up out of this, and the critical moment came when he was kneeling before the Blessed Sacrament begging God for his mercy. It was then, he said, that a great fog was lifted from his mind that brought a deep peace and consolation to him.

At eighteen, he enrolled at the University of Paris, the famous Sorbonne, where he excelled in his studies and was well known for his intellectual and oratorical abilities. Even in the anti-clerical bias, so prevalent in France, but worse in Paris itself, he was able to attract thousands to the Notre Dame Cathedral to listen to his lectures on faith.

He had organized a group of friends, who would meet regularly to discuss issues of faith and culture, which was always open to visitors interested in such issues. At one of these gatherings, one of the visitors chided him: "You people, who boast about being Catholics, where are the works that demonstrate your faith?" Ozanam knew in his heart that this student was right, and he talked to his closest friends as to how they could respond. What could they do? Out of this, of course, was the beginning of the St. Vincent de Paul Society.

His faith journey was soon to take a new direction. We have seen him as Son, as Man, and as Brother so far. At some point in his busy life of teaching and ministering to the poor, he considered what his vocation should be. He sincerely thought of priesthood, but decided that he wanted to serve God as a layman, and this decision was confirmed by his long time spiritual director, a priest who facilitated this move by arranging for a meeting with a young lady by the name of Amelie Soulacroix. It was love at first sight and they were soon married on June 23, 1841. It was a very happy marriage. After two miscarriages, Amelie gave birth to a daughter, Marie. Here is a quote from Ozanam's own words on this occasion: "A new blessing has come to me, perhaps the greatest joy that it is possible to experience here below! I am a father!" He took the role of fatherhood most seriously, as a call to greater holiness of life.

For the next eight years, he continued to multiply his works of charity and teaching, even establishing a newspaper for the purpose of promoting social justice. By the time he turned forty he was exhausted and in pain, brought on by the chronic disease that eventually ended in death. During his last year he used that time to grow closer to God. One day, when his priest friend was visiting he encouraged him to trust in God. His response was simply: "Why should I fear God, I love him so!"

Even during this period he penned a manual of scriptures and reflections, for those suffering from sickness and disease, called the "Bible of the Sick!" To the very end of his life, which occurred on September 8, 1853, he was the servant who cared for those in need.

I share this wonderful story with you because, in his dedication to God he marks the path that every real man should follow. He had the blessing of a wonderful father that would image for him his heavenly Father; he knew what it was and what it meant to be a son who was loved; he very quickly sprouted into manhood in such a home, and was arrayed with all those archetypal qualities we've been reflecting on.

Both, as warrior and adventurer, he risked a lot to attack the anti-clericalism and rationalism of post revolutionary France. His war against poverty in the streets of Paris was always a risky adventure. As a rescuer of beauty, he worked hard to present the best side of Holy Mother Church, the beauty created by his deep faith. As a man of a family, he was attentive to the needs of his wonderful wife and beautiful daughter. Frederic lived almost every moment of his life in possession of his deep masculine heart. He knew what it was to be a man. What a gift he has been to the Church. He was truly a man of God, a saint.

Sainthood is the ultimate goal for every man. This is the stage represented by the "sage" archetype. As a man slows down to contemplate his own final passing into the embrace of his heavenly Father, he is at the same time a well of wisdom and advice for others, who are on their own way through all the other stages of the journey. With all the emphasis on youthfulness today, the wisdom of the elderly is all too often ignored to the detriment of the youth and of the culture itself. In our next reflection we shall see how that wisdom was institutionalized from the beginning of human society.

REFLECTION X

PATRIARCHY

A prevailing theme in the long history of humankind on our planet, the one that seems to hold the vast array of experiences and changes in some kind of unity is called patriarchy. I begin this reflection with a recent model of an authentic patriarch.

Some time before Pope John Paul II died, I had the pleasure of reading his biography by George Weigel. This is a ponderous tome -- almost one thousand pages. And yet, it was not that difficult a project as it turned out. I really enjoyed the book. There were many discoveries and insights, both about the Holy Father himself, and the Church in which we live and worship. It is well worth the time it takes to read it.

The vision of the Holy Father included three very fundamental elements: first, the value and dignity of the human person; secondly, the call to unity within the body of Christ; and thirdly, outreach to the world's poor. These concerns are at the heart of almost everything that John Paul had said or written in his twenty-seven years as the head of our church.

One way he employed to carry his message to the world, was through his pastoral visits. He was the most traveled Pope in history...he had spoken to more people... he had visited more countries. He was indeed a man on the go, but on the go for Christ, with whom he had a deep and abiding relationship. Often as we experienced these visits, on the news of NBC or CNN, we noted the huge crowds that attended these events. Quite often this occurred in countries or places where there is no significant Christian presence, but somehow this man seemed to appeal to everyone. Why? I have often asked myself that question.

Some years ago there was a piece on the NBC News Report one evening about the Holy Father in connection with events in St. Louis. Part of the presentation included the comment, "that while many people, and particularly Catholics, revere and admire the Holy Father...a vast majority of them do not agree with his message." Well, then, we ask, why do they even bother to come to these events?

Deep within every human being is the need for a father. What Pope John Paul presented to the world was the image and model of authentic fatherhood - a man of principle - a man of compassion and understanding - and a man of deep faith. These are qualities every father must exhibit, if he is to influence his family and the society in which he lives. The Holy Father presented this kind of image and people flocked to him for that experience, the experience of *Patriarchy*.

I wish to reflect on that for a while, because this is one of my chief concerns in our world today - namely, the fatherless society in which we are living. Referring ourselves once again to the 1960's and 1970's . . . one of the victims of that revolution was, of course, patriarchy. And its demise was fueled very much by the women's movement - the feminist phenomenon. As women reflected on their own experiences of pain and suffering, regarding the fathers in their lives, they jumped to the conclusion that patriarchy was the chief cause of all their pain. Their pain, though, arises from the inappropriate and sinful behavior of patriarchs, who by their fault-filled lives, discredit the institution they were supposed to represent and honor. As we so often do, the women "discarded the baby with the bath water." They not only threw out the men, but they threw out the very institution that holds society together.

Look back through the long history of mankind, which goes back tens of thousands of years, and you will discover that it was the family, the clan, the tribe with the headship of its father, that preserved life, that supported life in the family and the tribe, but also encouraged discovery and exploration, and new ways of doing simple tasks around the family hearth or home.

Throughout the centuries, we saw the great patriarchs like Abraham, Isaac and Jacob, Moses and Aaron, David and Solomon . . . called to govern and unify the chosen people of God. In the Christian dispensation, we experienced great Fathers in the "Fathers of the Church" but more so in people like Benedict and the Monastic movement; Francis and the renewal of the thirteenth Century; Ignatius and Dominic, and Vincent de Paul...the great patriarchs of the religious orders that have arisen in the church in her long history.

But, the life of faith and church depended as much on the familial patriarch in the homes of Christians everywhere. The father of the family held the family together, was its social and economic provider, and also its moral and spiritual leader. As long as these fathers performed their roles according to Christian values and ideals, families were healthy and progressive. But, as well we know, men are prone to the seven capitol sins like every one else. So in some circumstances, the patriarch did not do his job very well, and all too often, very badly.

What we need to remember here is that it was not the institution that failed, but the individual father, or patriarch that failed. We do this all the time, we confuse the person with the institution. When members or leaders fail in their respective roles, then we want to discard the institution, rather than reforming the individuals. We see that so often in such comments as, "I don't go to church, because all those folks are hypocrites," or people have opined that they left the church because of the sin or failure of a priest or religious. The president of a college, the chief of police, the coach of a ball team, and many other social roles provide the opportunity of exercising a leadership with patriarchal energy. When their leadership role is exercised in a way that offers compassion and concern, not only for those whom they direct or command, but for the public they serve as well, that would be patriarchy, because the approach is that of a father to all those people.

Jesus came into the world to renew mankind, and part of that renewal was to renew the institution of patriarchy. And so he said to Peter: "You are rock, and upon this rock I will build my church. To you I give the keys of the kingdom of heaven, that whatsoever you loose upon earth, shall be loosed in heaven, and whatsoever you bind upon earth shall be bound in heaven..." (Matt. 16:18-19) But then, after Easter what does he say again to Peter: "Do you love me . . . then, tend my lambs, care for my sheep." (John 21:15-17) There we see the patriarchal vocation to which Peter is now called and which he must now exercise. It is this aspect of the Papal ministry that John Paul II took seriously. His whole life was a patriarchal ministry, and for twenty-seven years as the Pope he consistently fed the sheep and cared for the lambs. It is this dedication to his role as Father that attracted people...even his harshest critics. Because deep down within each human person is that "need" to have a father to go to. Somewhere I heard the little story about the youngster who said, "I want a god with skin on...", we know that Jesus was the God with skin on. But when we talk about God, as Father...we do not understand the meaning of that reality, unless we can experience it in a father with skin. And that is what John Paul II provided for his lambs and his sheep, and many others not of this fold - a father image, an authentic and faithful patriarch.

In the spring of 2005, it was announced that Pope John Paul was failing, and it appeared that the final chapter of his life here was about to be closed. CNN was already in Rome keeping us here in the states well informed. As the hours rolled by, crowds began to gather in the piazza before St. Peter's, and below the Papal apartments in the Apostolic Palace.

Finally late Saturday, on the eve of Divine Mercy Sunday, the news was finally released that his holiness had passed away. More crowds! Now we waited to learn when and how he would be buried. It was finally announced that it would be on Friday, April 8. I was utterly amazed at the way CNN handled this event. The very fact that they were there night and day during the illness, the death, the funeral, and during the period of mourning was a remarkable service to the people of America. And of course, they continued to be there, as the Cardinals prepared for and entered into the Conclave on April 18. Whether they intended it or not, or even if they knew it or not, CNN had provided a great service to the church.

The secular media was stunned, I am quite certain, at the vast sea of humanity that poured into the city of Rome, and eventually into the Piazza, and remained there throughout the entire ordeal, many of them even sleeping there during the cold nights. The reporters took advantage of this, of course, and milled about the crowds and interviewed any number of the pilgrims. It was astounding how many of them, when asked the question, "why did you come?" responded that they loved and admired the Holy Father. He was kind, he was warm, gentle, humorous, and compassionate.

To me many "whys" were left unasked. Why did you love him? Why did you admire him so much?

John Paul II stood before the world, and in the world, as a giant "Father" figure. And they had come to be with their father in his dying and in his funeral. The family of the Church, and even the family of mankind, looked upon John Paul as a great Patriarch — a giant father. Again, why? Because the world today, more than ever before, is lost in a vast network of fatherlessness. Mankind is searching for a real father, and Pope John Paul was that icon, that model, the paradigm of their search. Again, another why? Let me suggest two reasons, among others. First, his warmth, his gentleness, his compassion, and his friendliness, especially for the poor, the weak, the young, and the suffering. Secondly, he was a man who lived by principle and stood firmly on those principles. These are attributes really desired in a father: a man of principle and a man of compassion and understanding.

John Paul was every ounce a Pastor, and pastors need to go visit the people, which is what he did by traveling to every corner of the globe during his twenty seven years of papal ministry. And in those pastoral visits he reached out to all, but especially to the poor, the weak, the youth, and those suffering from hatred and violence. He knew his people and they certainly felt that they knew him, as has been testified to by the great crowds that had come to Rome, both to be with him as he died, and to say farewell to him at his funeral rite.

When I wrote these lines we were in the period of mourning and of waiting. Unlike so many Americans today, the Church believes in taking its time to mourn and only then to move on. This would put a formal and very spiritual closure to the life and service of this great priest of God.

Then came the waiting, as the church entered into a formal period of mourning. For nine days the college of cardinals paused in prayer and Eucharist to prepare themselves for the task of selecting an able successor to John Paul II. For twenty-seven years, this Polish priest had manned the ship of Peter amidst some very stormy seas. And now we waited for the naming of the new captain, a new patriarch.

Late in the afternoon of April 19, a Tuesday, the tell-tale white smoke issued from the chimney atop the Vatican and the bells of the Basilica of St. Peter began their joyous pealing. "Habemus Papam" Cardinal Estevez announces from the balcony. Joseph Cardinal Ratzinger had been selected by his brothers to succeed John Paul II. There was no need for the media to search for information about this man. He was already well known for his work as a trusted advisor to John Paul, and as the Prefect of the Congregation for the Doctrine of the Faith. In that role, he was often mischaracterized by the media, both public and religious, as an unyielding conservative, even lacking in compassion and understanding of the modern age. Now, as he entered into a new role in the Church, a pastoral role, his task will be much different, and I am certain that he will fulfill that call as diligently as he did in his previous assignment. He was 78 years old at that time! What a weighty burden to place on the shoulders of a man at this age of his life. I admire him for his surrender, not only to the will of the Cardinals, but to the Holy Spirit, that ever-present guardian of the Church. I know from my own reading, he is a man of God, a man of real prayer, and one in love with the Church that Christ has now bequeathed to him. I rather suspect that he will follow pretty much in the footsteps of his predecessor, and continue the great themes of that pontificate. He will exercise this awesome ministry as a true patriarch.

I digressed into this historical event simply to emphasize the deep seated need that humanity has for a real father. Unless we can recover and re-establish the patriarchal energy in our society, but most especially in our beleaguered homes, we will be rendered helpless in resolving the other issues confronting us today, such as terrorism, HIV/AIDS, and global warming.

FINAL REFLECTION

Like any other problem that seems to be so overwhelming, there is the temptation to despair and to simply give up. No one person, by himself, can resolve the issues we have presented in this book, but one person can make a difference by using his or her gifts in the milieu where he or she lives, works and plays. I have inserted a number of photos of fathers and sons, who, by their close relationship represents the importance of a father's presence in his son's life. Some of these have very young boys; others have adult males, who are beginning their own families. No matter how young or how old the boy may be, he still needs that father in his world.

This book was a formidable undertaking, but it has paid off in many ways even for my own personal understanding of who I am, and how events, relationships, and faith have influenced the journey I continue to walk. While most of the material arose out of my dissatisfaction, sometimes even anger at the political, social, and economic injustices and dissimulations, yet, I grew in my openness to the lessons or messages that lay behind each of them.

My own tendency to perfectionism, of course, frequently gets in the way of honest assessment of these events. And as I struggled to see the possible good in them I was forced to look into my own psychic geography, and look for that focus point that John Eldridge refers to as the "father wound."

My own father, generally, was a pretty laid back individual. He was a wonderful family man who took good care of us in the traditional ways that the culture of the time prescribed. As we know from thousands of years of experience, no man is perfect. We are flawed by a corrupted human nature. And so it was with my father.

My wound came to me in a single event. On this particular day I was instructed by my father as he left for work to be sure and clean the chicken coop. That was a task I absolutely detested – it was dirty and dusty and smelly – and so I kept putting it off, intending eventually to get it done before the last minute. My father, however, arrived home before that last minute. When he assessed the work in the chicken house and discovered it undone, he became undone, and in harsh anger shouted at me, ". . .you are the laziest damn kid that ever came down the pike!" That was an epithet that would color my life as I grew into adulthood. My father had corrected us on other occasions and even had punished us at times. This moment was different, whether for the intensity of my father's anger, or the abusive language, my heart was shattered, deeply wounded. Effects of this wounding ended up affecting my approach to life. It did not destroy the relationship between father and son, but it did color how I looked at work, not so much as a livelihood but as a means, even a weapon, to prove I was not lazy.

As I look back now, I can see that my perfectionism is rooted in those few words my father used that day. In my adult life, I have strived to prove to my father that I am not the "laziest" kid around, all of this, of course, was on the unconscious level. In addition to the perfectionism I have a strong work ethic. I am a constant "doer." I have a hard time sitting still and just being there, which of course is a hindrance to a deep prayer life, at which I have spent a lot of time and energy.

This book has been an exercise of "doing!" It continues to be a means by which, in my advancing years, I can still be busy about something worthwhile. However, it offers me in my "sage" years the opportunity to share, whatever wisdom and advice my journey has garnered along the way, with my brothers in the human family.

By the time you conclude the reading of this monograph on the relationship between fathers and sons, you will catch a few glimmers of hope along the way. Through my own ministry I have made contact with a number of men who are exercising their fatherhood both with their sons and their daughters in remarkable ways. Measured against the total population, these few examples may or may not create much hope for the future. In both my ministry and my travels, I find more and more examples that increase my own optimism with regard to this troubling issue.

Each one of the programs that I referred to in my Reflection on Hope, is that if they remain faithful to their mission, and persevering in their ministry, more fathers and sons will find the healing of that tell-tale "wound" leading them into a rediscovery of their masculine souls. You will probably not agree with some of my propositions and that is quite acceptable. I only wish that you will reflect on them with the eye and heart of faith.

It may be of assistance in our reflection on these issues to do so in the light of this beautiful ancient hymn, here presented in an English translation:

Creator of the earth and skies,
to whom all trust and power belong.
Grant us your truth to make us wise;
Grant us your power to make us strong.

We have not known you;
to the skies our monuments of folly soar,
and all our self-wrought miseries
have made us trust ourselves the more.

We have not loved you;
far and wide the wreckage of our hatred spreads,
and evils wrought by human pride
recoil on unrepentant heads.

We long to end this world wide strife;
how shall we follow in your way?
Speak to mankind your words of life,
until our darkness turns to day.

AUTHORS OF REFERENCE

Arnold, M. Patrick, <u>Wildmen, Warriors, and Kings - Masculine Spirituality and the Bible</u>, Crossroad Publishing Co. 1992

Bly, Robert, <u>Iron John - A Book About Men</u>, Random House, 1990

Carnes, Patrick, <u>Out of the Shadows</u>, CompCare Pub, 1983 "<u>Contrary to Love</u>, CompCare Pub. 1989

Carter, Jimmy, <u>Our Endangered Values</u>, Simon & Schuster, 2005

Dalbey, Gordon, <u>Father and Son - the Wound, the Healing, the Call to Manhood,</u> Thomas Nelson Pub. 1992   "Healing the Masculine Soul, Word Publishing 1988

Dobson, James and others, <u>Seven Promises of a Promise Keeper</u>, Focus on the Family Pub. 1994

Eldridge, John, <u>Wild at Heart</u>, Thomas Nelson Pub. 2001 "<u>The Way of the Wild Heart</u>, Nelson Books, 2006

Gerzon, Mark, <u>A Choice of Heroes, the Changing Face of American Manhood</u>, Houghton Mifflin Co.1982

Gurian, Michael, <u>A Fine Young Man</u>, Penguin/Putnam Inc. 1998

Hardenbrook, Weldon M., <u>Missing from Action -</u>

Vanishing Manhood in America, Thomas Nelson Pub., 1987

Keen, Sam, Fire in the Belly - on Being a Man, Bantam Books 1991

Meacham, Jon, American Gospel, Random House, 2006

Moberly, Elizabeth R. Homosexuality - a New Christian Ethic, James Clark & Co. "Psychogenesis - the early development of gender identity, Rutledge & Kegan Paul Ltd. 1983

Monick, Eugene, Phallos - Sacred Image of the Masculine, Inner City Books, 1987

Moore, Robert & Douglas Gillette, King, Warrior, Magician, Lover, Harper 1990

Nouwen, Henri J. M., The Way of the Heart, Harper-Collins Pub. 1981

Payne, Leanne Crisis in Masculinity, Crossway Books, 1985

Rohr, Richard & Joseph Martos, The Wild Man's Journey, St. Anthony Messenger Press, 1992

Rossetti, Stephen J., The Joy of Priesthood, Ave Maria Press, 2005

Ryan, Thomas, Wellness, Spirituality and Sports, Paulist Press 1986

Schaller, James L., The Search for Lost Fathering, Revell 1995

Steichen, Donna, Ungodly Rage - The Hidden Face of Catholic Feminism, Ignatius Press 1991

Summers, Christina Hoff, The War Against Boys, Simon & Schuster 2000

Wallis, Jim, God's Politics, Harper San Francisco, 2005

Weigel, George, Witness to Hope, Cliff Street Books 1999

Wyly, James, The Phallic Quest, Inner City Books, 1989

ACKNOWLEDGMENTS

At the beginning I must acknowledge the work of Marilyn Barnhardt who did a large part of the editorial work on this book. I will be ever grateful for that generous effort.

To Deanne and Jim Largess for their assistance and abiding attention to this project offering their suggestions and encouragement.

Sandy Lardinois of LifeVest Publishing supervised the design and layout of our book, the most involved person in this entire process and I am most grateful to her and to her team for their hard work.

Many families cooperated to provide me with the photos that were used in the text: 1) Mary Wheeler; 2) Jeanne Hall; 3) Barbara Brown; 4) Brian Dolan; 5) Tom Jenko; 6) John Kaney; 6) Zeke Kaney; 8) Rick Ahman; 9) Judy Gallagher; and finally, I received the "brotherhood" shot from a men's group here in my own locale.

To all the men who shared retreats, workshops, and cursillos with me over the years and provided both ideas and encouragement for this undertaking.

Tom, a doctor, and Sons in Bonding Events

To order copies of

RESCUING VANISHING MANHOOD

ISBN 1-59879-561-9

You may order on line at:
www.lifevestbooks.com

Order by phone at:
Toll Free
877-843-1007

Centennial, Colorado